PRAISE FOR

CHASING THE BRIGHT SIDE

"*Chasing the Bright Side* is essential reading for anyone facing a challenge, in work or in life. With emotion, humility, and humor (and some amazing stories), Jess Ekstrom not only demonstrates how anyone with a dream can eventually persevere, but also shows by example how we all can tap into the passion to do so. It's the book I wish I had read before starting my own entrepreneurial journey, but luckily it's not too late for everyone else. I'll be recommending this book to my own children, to the aspiring entrepreneurs I work with, and to everyone I meet who aspires to find more purpose in their life. It's a page-turner that you won't be able to put down until you've finished but holds lessons that will reveal themselves to you for a lifetime."
  —Marc Randolph, Netflix cofounder and first CEO

"Three things you can control in life are your attitude, your effort, and your actions. If you're ready to see challenges as opportunities for growth, *Chasing the Bright Side* is the guide you need."
  —Marie Forleo, author of *Everything Is Figureoutable*

"Optimism is never accidental. Jess Ekstrom knows this better than anyone. I love that she's given practical, encouraging, empowering steps to discovering what it takes to lead with optimism. Read this today if you want to change your tomorrow."
  —Jon Acuff, *New York Times* bestselling author of
  Finish: Give Yourself the Gift of Done

"Immerse yourself in Jess Ekstrom's entrepreneurial optimism and allow her remarkable journey to convince you page by page that you can achieve great things in business and life. Jess is one of my favorite girls—her big heart and self-taught tenacity touch thousands of people, making her a genuine hero to those she serves and a leader for the business community to emulate. I've jumped at every chance to feature Jess and her Headbands of Hope mission on national TV because it inspires everyone, regardless of circumstance, to chase the bright side."
  —Tory Johnson, *Good Morning America* contributor,
  New York Times bestselling author, and speaker

"There's no better way to transform your life than by transforming your mind-set. In *Chasing the Bright Side*, Jess Ekstrom will motivate you to believe that something better is possible and empower you to create lasting positive change. Optimism is a choice, and when you choose to embrace it, there's no limit to the good you can create in your life and in the world."

—Jack Canfield, coauthor of the *New York Times* bestselling *Chicken Soup for the Soul®* series and author of *The Success Principles™*

"Optimism is a daily choice. It's not naive or Pollyanna; it's a foundation for success in life. In *Chasing the Bright Side*, Jess Ekstrom will motivate you see your challenges as opportunities to learn and grow and believe the best is yet to come. Every day you can focus on being positive, working hard, and making others around you better, and Jess's inspiring message will help you get there."

—Jon Gordon, bestselling author of *The Energy Bus* and *The Power of Positive Leadership*

"Jess Ekstrom gives you a window into the soul of entrepreneurial optimism and tenacity in a way no other book does. Her transparency and humor will delight you and embolden you to believe that anything is possible."

—Nancy Duarte, CEO and bestselling author

"The key to your success is waiting for you inside the pages of Jess Ekstrom's new book, *Chasing the Bright Side*. She had me highlighting and nodding my head in agreement throughout the entire book. Jess's experience and writing style will have you doing the same. Your success needs an experienced cheerleader, and she's waiting for you in the pages of this book."

—Lindsay Teague Moreno, entrepreneur, speaker, and author of *Boss Up!*

"Jess Ekstrom exudes what it means to be a Catalyst leader. She's a true hope dealer and is inspiring a new generation of change-makers. *Chasing the Bright Side* is not just a great book; it's a lifestyle manifesto! If you're looking to be inspired, filled up with hope, and raise your overall optimism quotient, read this book!"

—Brad Lomenick, former president of Catalyst and author of *The Catalyst Leader* and *H3 Leadership*

"Jess Ekstrom's *Chasing the Bright Side* will empower you to step up, take risks, and learn by doing. With humor and admirable transparency about her missteps, Jess will inspire you to live with purpose and do important work that has a profound impact on those around you."

—Kristen Hadeed, author of *Permission to Screw Up* and founder of Student Maid™

"We often believe we need grit or perseverance to overcome our struggles and our failure, but optimism is the secret ingredient to true success. Jess's inspiring story of resilience and positivity shows us that true optimism is possible, even in our darkest hours. *Chasing the Bright Side* is a realistic look at how we can shift our mind-set to see the positive and live a life that feels happier."

—Tonya Dalton, author of *The Joy of Missing Out* and CEO of inkWELL Press Productivity Co.

"Full disclosure: I am a huge Jess Ekstrom fan! I have seen firsthand her passion, impact, and joy for changing the lives of all she serves. *Chasing the Bright Side* is more than a blueprint for creating a social and business impact for new and existing leaders; it is a map to changing the world."

—Ron Kitchens, CEO of Southwest Michigan First and author of *Uniquely You* and *Community Capitalism*

CHASING THE BRIGHT SIDE

CHASING THE BRIGHT SIDE

EMBRACE *Optimism,*
ACTIVATE YOUR *Purpose,*
AND *Write Your Own Story*

Jess Ekstrom

W Publishing Group

AN IMPRINT OF THOMAS NELSON

Published in Nashville, Tennessee, by W Publishing, an imprint of Thomas Nelson.

Published in association with Yates & Yates, www.yates2.com.

Thomas Nelson titles may be purchased in bulk for educational, business, fund-raising, or sales promotional use. For information, please e-mail SpecialMarkets@ ThomasNelson.com.

Any Internet addresses, phone numbers, or company or product information printed in this book are offered as a resource and are not intended in any way to be or to imply an endorsement by Thomas Nelson, nor does Thomas Nelson vouch for the existence, content, or services of these sites, phone numbers, companies, or products beyond the life of this book.

ISBN 978-0-7852-2931-5 (eBook)

Library of Congress Control Number: 2019901085

ISBN 978-0-7852-2932-2

Printed in the United States of America

19 20 21 22 23   LSC   10 9 8 7 6 5 4 3 2 1

For my mom, Laurie, the unsinkable optimist

CONTENTS

INTRODUCTION

Hi, I'm Jess. I'm a rowdy sports fan disguised as a polite Southern girl. I'm obsessed with my dog (and my husband is pretty great too). I'm an entrepreneur with no business plan. I laugh at my own jokes. I can't touch my toes. I don't own an iron. I think I'm the only person who can't keep a succulent alive, and I'm always on the hunt for my next burrito bowl.

But before we dive in, I think it's important you know some of my core beliefs:

- French fries don't have calories if they're on someone else's plate.
- Thrift shopping counts as exercise.
- If you bring your umbrella, it won't rain.
- Coffee goes toward your daily water intake.
- Menus with pictures help me make more informed ordering decisions.
- My dog completely understands when I speak to him in full sentences.
- Yellow traffic lights mean you floor it.
- Airports are rated by their food courts and seat-to-outlet ratio.
- Picking up your takeout order on a Friday night still qualifies as "going out."

Now that we've been acquainted, I want you to know I'm glad you're here. Whether you're curled up in your favorite chair with a cup of coffee, or you're standing in a bookstore holding three different titles and wondering if *this* book is worthy of your precious time, here's a quick peek at what this journey will be like.

This book will have lots of stories (good, great, funny, bad—and really bad) of how I've created a company that's helped hundreds of thousands of kids with cancer. I've been able to share this mission on shows like the *Today Show*, *Good Morning America*, and *The View*. Celebrities like Lauren Conrad, Kelsea Ballerini, Khloé Kardashian, and Lea Michele have marched behind it. And we've now donated hundreds of thousands of headbands to children with cancer in dozens of different countries.

But inside all these stories is one consistent thread, and it's the thread that you'll learn to practice as you read this book: *optimism*. Why optimism? Because anyone who has ever done something great had to believe in something better than the present.

As you read, you'll see that optimism isn't about getting from A to B. Optimism is this rooted belief that there's something good on the other side. It's about the voice in our heads that gives us the green light to chase our dreams. It's about understanding that we can't control all of our experiences, but we can control what they mean to us and the story they write for us. (I'll give you the tools to help you do just that.)

The stories we write from our experiences help us decide:

- If we're going to start the business—or not.
- If we're going to attempt the pull-up—or not.
- If we're going to pick up the trash on the street—or not.
- If we're going to ask for the promotion—or not.
- If we're going to book that trip—or not.
- If we're going to live fulfilled—or not.

The stories we write in our heads tell us how we're going to respond. Are we good enough? Tall enough? Up for the challenge? Is it the "right" time?

But sometimes the voices in our heads tell us it's not our turn, or they make us believe we're not ready. If we listen in those moments, it's easy to get knocked off track. So what happens when we choose to change the story?

Opportunity. That's what happens when we move beyond those negative voices and change the narrative to focus on the possibility that there's good out there—and we can bring it into reality. It opens up a whole other world that we might have thought was beyond reach.

Everything we want is within our grasp if we're willing to throw perfection out the door and embrace the messiness of the journey. Isn't it crazy to think that the entire life we want is waiting for us on the other side of our thoughts? One flicker of change inside our heads can catapult us onto the stage we were born to stand on.

Now, just to clarify: this book is not a positivity pledge.

I'm not going to tell you to put on a happy face and skip down the street high-fiving everyone who walks by. (Although, if you want to do that, I'm not stopping you.) I'm not going to tell you to just add sprinkles and everything will be okay. And I'm certainly not going to tell you, "Don't worry, be happy" because I think someone already said that.

Optimism is that place where we can see and understand the bad but still believe there can be good. And most important, optimism fuels the belief that *we* can be the ones to create the good the world needs.

If you peel back the layers of anyone's success, optimism is the first seed that has to be planted for any great movement, change, start-up, or revolution to begin. A lot of the time, we think this seed is a skill set or expertise, so we don't go for it. As if anyone who joins the circus was born knowing how to swing from the trapeze or jump through fire. None of us was born knowing how to fly a plane, do our taxes, poach an egg, or start a company. We all had to start somewhere. And that "somewhere" is optimism.

So, let's debunk this myth that to be successful you have to have it all figured out, because that's impossible. In order for us to have a chance at making a dent in the universe, we have to be optimistic enough to see something better and confident enough to just begin. We grow and learn on the way to our goals, not in the static planning.

I started Headbands of Hope when I was nineteen years old. It was a college dorm room start-up and as scrappy as they come. For every headband sold, a headband is donated to a child with cancer. Making that happen has been some of the most rewarding, impactful work I could have imagined.

It all started with a summer internship at the Make-A-Wish Foundation—with the belief that there has to be good in the middle of the hard stuff, and maybe I can be the one to create it. Well, that's the cookie-cutter, podcast-interview, LinkedIn-bio, let's-meet-for-coffee-and-brag-about-ourselves answer that I always give—but it's only a small part of the story.

I wasn't skipping around in a flower crown when an idea popped into my head. Optimism came from feeling like I was being dragged down a river, then found a branch I could grab to help me stay afloat. I white-knuckled on to meaning and purpose when I felt like I was out of control and being pulled underwater. Maybe we can see the good more clearly when we need it most.

Sometimes optimism can be hard because we have to progressively think about things that haven't even happened yet. We have to let ourselves dream of a better *next*. But the threat of not being optimistic is stagnancy. We can't move forward to a better tomorrow if we don't believe and visualize what could be. Then we must be confident enough to actively march toward that vision.

This book will share moments of my life when I didn't just magically find the bright side; I had to chase it. Whether that was with my business, my family, or even becoming a water aerobics instructor (yes, I'm serious)—when I didn't just magically find the bright side; I had to chase it.

Optimism is the combination of how you think, how you react, and how you connect your life to something greater. Living optimistically will set you up for a wild and meaningful life, but if you're one of those people who needs science and data to believe something is important, then pretend Bill Nye the Science Guy is narrating this part:

- "The Mayo Clinic reports a number of health benefits associated with optimism, including a reduced risk of death from cardiovascular problems, less depression, and an increased life span."[1]
- *Harvard Men's Health Watch* says, "Optimism helps people cope with disease and recover from surgery. Even more impressive is the impact of a positive outlook on overall health and longevity. Research tells us that an optimistic outlook early in life can predict better health and a lower rate of death during follow-up periods of fifteen to forty years."[2]
- The National Center for Biotechnology Information says, "Optimists are significantly more successful than pessimists in aversive events and when important life-goals are impaired."[3]

Are you convinced now?

This book will not force you to be happier or make you feel like you're not doing enough. I'm tired of lists that guarantee happiness if I just drink more water and meditate at red lights.

I am not going to judge you or make you feel guilty. What I want is to motivate and inspire you to chase the one life you have been given. I'm here to help you train a muscle in your head to see the good (even when it's hard) and give you the extra push to create your own beautiful reality. This book will show that you can understand and absorb negativity without being consumed by it. It's time to forge your own way and create the life you want to live.

Optimism opens the door to the pastures of possibility that are there for all of us if we just look for them. Trust me, it's there for you.

So, let's stop with the Sunday scaries and say *yes* to life's offer to live loud, vibrantly, and purposefully.

Life is short, and so is my attention span. Fill up your coffee cup, and let's get started!

EVERYING *wonderful* THAT HAS BEEN CREATED OR ACHIEVED HAD TO START WITH SOMEONE WHO *believed* IT COULD BE *better.*

#chasingthebrightside

One

MAYBE SHE'S BORN WITH IT

*She refused to be bored, chiefly
because she wasn't boring.*
—ZELDA FITZGERALD

In middle school you could probably detect my braces from outer space. I was the kid who opened her mouth in the chair at the orthodontist and they had to call for backup. Every tooth had a lever or chain attached to another tooth, and they were all in this together. My teeth were like, *Hang in there, Jess. We've got this. Just don't eat popcorn.*

Braces were awkward and painful, but I was so thrilled when my mom told me I was getting them. This is because:

1. I got to pick the band color, and I had been working up color schemes for a while.
2. I was one step closer to a beautiful, straight-toothed smile.

I was not naive about my desperate need for braces. Every day I looked in the mirror and could see I needed a dental intervention. Even though I knew braces would be uncomfortable and I might look funny for a few years, I honestly didn't care. Braces meant I was working toward something better. Braces meant progress toward a beautiful smile, and I was ready for change. Braces were my optimism.

As kids, we're just four feet of optimism walking into everything we do like we're going to win, because sometimes we haven't experienced enough to tell us that we might lose. And sometimes as kids our optimism is so strong that we skillfully find the good even in the not-so-great moments.

My optimism really lit up when I took on the official role of match-maker.

During recess I would play basketball with the boys while all the girls hung out on the swing set. Before recess I'd talk to the girls and see which boys they were interested in so I could get the scoop on the basketball court.

> Claire: Can you ask Harrelson if he wants to be partners on the Language Arts project?
> Lindsey: I know Timmy asked Rebecca to the dance, but we brushed elbows in Social Studies, so I feel like he definitely likes me now. Can you find out for me?

It was like taking orders before I went to Taco Bell. "Okay, who likes who? Who wants what? You want that hot, medium, or mild?"

This was my way of creating my place in the social hierarchy. I'd play matchmaker so I had some social role to offer the girls' group. Then I'd skip off to basketball and extract the information I needed from the boys. "Hey, Timmy. Are you emotionally available right now?"

My favorite part was after recess when we all lined up to go back into school because that's when all the girls would run up to me and I could report my findings. You know, make myself useful. I would rattle off today's digs:

> Jess: Timmy's hamster just died; he's still coping. Kendrick would like to ask Sarah or Becca to the dance. Either one

is fine, he said. Ryan is looking for someone who can
dunk from the free-throw line.

And for just a brief moment, all eyes were on me. For some reason, I never really made the connection that none of the boys were asking *me* out. I wasn't girly enough to be in the girl groups or boyish enough to be in the boy groups, so I was the medium in between. I was the match-maker; I created my own value and purpose. And that was good enough for me.

CHILDLIKE OPTIMISM

When we are kids, we have this innate optimism within ourselves about what could be. We're this blank slate of possibility that has yet to be told there's anything we can't do.

You want to go to the moon? Sit under the stars and plan your route.

You want to be a dolphin trainer? Here's your whistle.

You want to start a restaurant that serves only Jell-O? Buy hundreds of those tiny boxes and get mixing.

Nothing is off-limits because we haven't experienced limits yet. We haven't been told what's impossible. We haven't equated our scraped knees to our self-worth. We haven't been told our chances are low. We haven't danced with the thought of failure. As kids, we're purely moving as we are because we haven't been told what to be.

And when we're in that headspace, we move. We take risks, we jump, and we leap because the consequences of it "not working out" are not in our vocabulary yet.

Imagine what you would do right now if the chance of failure didn't cross your mind.

For me in middle school, that meant chasing this other dream of mine. When I got confident in my matchmaking abilities, I decided to experiment with another personal passion: writing. More specifically, writing something to be published in *Chicken Soup for the Soul*.

Maybe the goals of most sixth-grade girls are going out with a boy, making a sports team, or trying not to make their viola squeak. For me, I was in the friend zone with boys basically until college, and I couldn't try out for sports teams until seventh grade, so *Chicken Soup for the Soul* seemed like a natural fit in terms of lifelong dreams. It all started when the "popular" girls would get copies of the book and sit in a circle during recess and discuss the stories, like a modern-day book club minus the wine and cheese or any sort of real-life experience to draw from. I'd overhear them saying lines like:

- "I couldn't believe he went *back* for his pony after so much time had passed!"
- "I feel like her struggle was what really made her find her strength."
- "After all those years, her twin sister was just right around the corner. Who knew?!"

I would run over from the basketball court, hot and sweaty and ignorant of the concept of body odor, and plop down at the edge of their circle, desperate to be in the conversation. Luckily, I was usually wearing a skort, so it was functional for basketball *and* book club.

Side note: all in favor of skorts making a comeback? *Me!*

I realized that in order for me to stand a chance in the popular group, I had to read *Chicken Soup for the Soul*. So, after school I told my mom I wanted to run by the bookstore and grab a copy. This was a surprise because typically my after-school requests centered around ice cream or any other kind of food.

That night I started reading the book, and I had a revelation: these are *real* people in this book. Real people submit their stories to *Chicken Soup for the Soul*. I'm a real person, which means—I can be in this book.

I felt like Elle Woods deciding she was going to go to Harvard. *Imagine what the popular girls would think of me if I didn't just read the book, I was in the book?* The thought of me arriving in the carpool line via limousine with all the kids begging me to autograph their books flashed in my head. My driver would hand me my lunch, which would be chicken fingers and waffle fries, and give me a nod in the rearview mirror before I stepped out into an overwhelming sea of middle schoolers begging for my attention.

I found the submission address in the back of the book and immediately got to writing. Every day I felt like I was J. K. Rowling writing what happens next in Harry Potter. I borrowed envelopes and stamps from my dad, and he taught me where the stamp and the return label go on a letter. I probably submitted close to one hundred writing submissions. No exaggeration.

During lunch I'd write poems, and my English teacher, Mrs. Strickland, would look them over. Did my writing carry enough emotional weight for a twelve-year-old? This was honestly my biggest concern—bigger than the concern that I would actually make it in the book. If I just kept submitting work, no matter how long it took, I knew I'd make it in there because that's how the story goes. You try, try, and try again, and then you eventually make it. That's the formula, so I kept writing.

One day I came home from school, and my mom told me I got a letter. She handed me the envelope, and three things went through my mind:

1. *I never get mail; this is awesome!*
2. *What kind of snack should I eat as I open this?*
3. *Oh my gosh! It's from* Chicken Soup for the Soul*!*

I opened up the envelope as my mom sat there grinning from ear to ear. The best thing about my mom is, no matter what you do, she acts like you were just called onstage at the Oscars for winning Best Actor. Her reactions when I first made it on the *Today Show* versus winning a scratch-off lottery card for ten dollars were actually quite similar: both ecstatic.

My eyes skimmed the opening paragraph: "Congratulations! Your work has been chosen to be in *Chicken Soup for the Soul: Teenage Edition*. Enclosed is your check for seventy-five dollars for your winning submission."

Now here was what was going through my mind:

1. *I did it!*
2. *Just wait until the popular girls hear about this.*
3. *Teenage?! I'm only twelve! I'm so ahead of my time.*
4. *Seventy-five dollars should cover my college tuition, right?*

My mom and I jumped up and down in the kitchen, holding the letter above my head and screaming like we were at an 'NSYNC concert. This was it. After nearly a hundred failed attempts, I had hit the dartboard.

To celebrate, my mom and I went to the local American Eagle so I could buy a new outfit to wear to school the next day. I wanted to make sure I looked like Heidi Klum walking down those hallways with all the attention I was going to get. I remember the outfit we picked out like it was yesterday: cargo bell-bottom pants with snap pockets on the side. The real kicker was that it came with a colorful sash for the belt that hung off the side like an Avril Lavigne "Sk8ter Boi" video. Then we got a lime green long-sleeve top to match the hue in the sash. I know, I was killing it.

My mom dropped me off at school, and I busted through those double doors like a lawyer walking into court with evidence that will win the case. I gripped my acceptance letter in my left hand and rolled my roller backpack with my right.

The first thing I did was show Mrs. Strickland the letter. She was thrilled and walked me up to the principal's office so I could be on the morning announcements and share my fame with all of Davidson Middle School. I felt like I was appearing on MTV announcing my latest album . . . dropping *now!*

After the morning announcements and classes started to change, I walked down that hall with the confidence of a poker player with a royal flush, my side sash swaying in the wind. I imagined the people staring at me were saying, "Look! It's the girl who's in *Chicken Soup for the Soul: Teenage Edition!*"

That afternoon at recess I grabbed my letter (now wrinkled) and brought it to show the girls in book club. I moved my sash onto my lap so it didn't get grass stains. I held my letter up to the group and said, "Well, ladies. Grab the newest *Chicken Soup* and flip to page 231 because you'll find *me!*"

I waited for the eruption of applause or the high fives or the invitations to sleepovers, but they never came.

"That's nice, but we've moved on to Judy Blume," one of them said.

This is the part where I'm supposed to tell you I was devastated and felt like I did all that work for nothing. But to be honest, I don't remember feeling that. Despite their reactions, I was still soaring knowing I did something that I set my mind to.

Their reaction didn't stop me from taking a trip to Barnes & Noble and manually moving the book to the best sellers table, having my mom take a picture of me beside it, and putting that as my Myspace profile picture. Their reaction didn't stop me from autographing copies and putting it in the locker of any boy I had a crush on. Their reaction didn't stop me from doing my own book tour around my neighborhood cul-de-sac. Their reaction didn't stop me from reaching out to our local newspaper to tell them they should do a story on my young success—which they did. Their reaction did not stop me from being proud of myself for accomplishing what I worked so hard to accomplish—I was in control of that, and so are you.

THROWING DARTS

Despite the reactions of the "popular girls" (whom I never was accepted by, thank goodness), I had shattered my own glass ceiling. I realized the formula for getting what you want: it doesn't matter how many times you miss; you just have to make it once. I could just keep throwing darts until I finally hit something.

And that's the beauty of childlike optimism: we have this fearless approach to pursuing the good and a never-ending list of what's possible. Having a childlike and optimistic mind-set is like a table with LEGOS dumped on it. We can focus on the mess and disorder, or we can focus on what we can build and the fun of creating something new.

Most of us have a blind optimism when we're younger. Our pros and cons lists are only pros because we don't know the cons. We are floating through life, waiting for our braces to come off. We don't think too long or hard about what might go wrong. We just walk through what life throws at us. We simply go for it and see what happens.

But then something happens that pops our balloon.

It usually happens when we're a little bit older. Something makes us become aware of our limits, and our humanness scares us into thinking we cannot do what we actually can. We become aware of the watching world around us, and we become self-conscious about failing in front of it. Suddenly every poem that doesn't get accepted to *Chicken Soup* is a reflection on us. Or we wonder what it would look like if we tried out for the basketball team and didn't make it. We start watering the weeds instead of the flowers. We feel fear. Our confidence is rattled. And we slowly stop believing.

Maybe it's studying really hard for a test, and someone who cheated gets a better grade than you. Or maybe it's a boy who breaks your heart. Or maybe it's not getting into your dream college. The more things don't go your way, the more you question the template you've been told is supposed to work in life:

- Work hard = get paid.
- Be nice = make friends.
- Study = get good grades.
- Eat your veggies = be skinny.

Something makes you realize your life equations don't add up like they used to. Something makes it hard to remember who you were before you were told what to be.

This disruption can happen on a different timeline for everyone. The kink in the hose, the snag in the sweater, the skip in the record. Something makes us question *if* there is good in the world.

For me, this disruption was senior year of high school.

Take It or Leave It ....

Think about a time when you were focused only on the pros instead of the cons.

- What could go *right*?
- Was it when you were a kid, or have you felt that recently?
- When was a time in your life that you were persistent?
- What was it about what you wanted that kept you going?

WE CAN'T *control* OUR EXPERIENCES, BUT WE CAN ALWAYS *write* OUR STORIES.

#chasingthebrightside

Two

ANYTHING CAN HAPPEN

You will have bad times, but they will always wake
you up to the stuff you weren't paying attention to.
—ROBIN WILLIAMS

Growing up, I had a pretty awesome childhood. The worst thing that
happened to me was my goldfish, Albert, jumped out of his bowl and
my mom accidentally stepped on him. We hosted a proper memorial,
but Mom still can't look at goldfish to this day, which is under-
standable.

Other than that, my family was pretty normal. Our vacations were
always camping. (Our first dog's name was Camper. That's how hard-
core we were.) Our family reunions were usually pretty tame, with the
exception of the one when the adults decided to hire a guy who had a
bunch of random animals (red flag #1), and he brought those animals to
the backyard and a tarantula got loose. He claimed it was all a part of the
act, but to this day, twenty years later, I don't buy it.

The normalcy of my childhood makes the story I'm about to tell that
much harder to process. Because no one saw it coming.

It was 2008, and the economy was rough, but Brad and Angelina
were still together. The iPhone was barely a year old and Instagram wasn't

invented yet. Britney Spears had made her comeback. Bey and Jay got married. Life was going okay.

I was around seventeen years old, so all that was on my mind was hoping I was going to go to a college that had cute boys, and wondering what "away" message I was going to put up on my AOL Instant Messenger.

It was early December, exam week. I'm not very skilled at standardized tests no matter how much I studied, so I was already a bit on edge. I was the student who worked her booty off in order to be average. Plus, the school I was at was a smaller private school that made me believe life's biggest decisions were going to be in an A, B, C, or D formula, and I needed to get my head on straight if I wanted a chance at a white picket fence and golden retriever.

On the morning of my English exam, I walked downstairs to be fed a breakfast of champions before my test. My parents are health nuts, so my whole life I was programmed to believe that breakfast is a necessity to function at your highest potential. Not having breakfast was like pulling out of the driveway for a cross-country road trip with no gas. So, I was confused when there wasn't any breakfast. Also, the morning news wasn't on. That was our morning tradition: eat breakfast and have the news playing in the background as we talk about our upcoming day. My mom looked like she had been crying, and my dad looked like he was in a fog. My parents are the happiest people I know, so this was not a state I had ever seen them in.

When my mom saw me come downstairs, she quickly went to the cabinet and brought out some cereal and milk, not making eye contact with me.

"Is everything okay?" I said.

"Everything is fine," my dad said. "We'll talk about it after your exams."

That didn't sit right with me. My parents are usually open and honest about *everything*. When I got my first boyfriend, my mom pulled out her yearbook and walked me through all of *her* past boyfriends and why they didn't work out. So anytime my parents were quiet about something, it had to be bad.

"I'd like to know now," I said. "I won't be able to focus on my exams if I know something is wrong."

My mom left the room, and my dad walked over to the countertop I was sitting at and looked me in the eyes. He said, "Things are going to be different around here. We lost all of our money, so our lifestyle is going to change a bit. But we're going to be okay."

I'll be honest, being told that we lost all of our money didn't hit me over the head with a shovel or anything. I knew that was a *very* bad thing, but I didn't have a good enough grasp on finances (or even a good enough grasp on reality) to know what that meant.

My dad said we could talk more about it later and just to not tell anyone at school. He also said to stay away from the news, which I didn't understand. But I said okay and gave him and my mom each a hug good-bye and walked to my car.

I don't really remember anything else about that day. I assume I did fine on my exam, since I eventually went to college and I think I turned out okay. But I do remember the uneasiness I felt. I felt like I knew the results of something but not the trigger. Like I saw a broken window but not the rock that shattered it.

That evening I got home and went into the guest room that was down a hallway near the garage, where my parents wouldn't realize I was home or hear the TV. I turned on the news, and that's when I saw it.

My uncle's face. On every national news channel.

Uncle Bernie Madoff.

Every channel had faces of Bernie Madoff and other members of our family. I couldn't even hear what the news was saying. I just stared at the television with a loud buzzing in my ear and my head feeling light. Eventually, bits and pieces of information started to filter through:

- Bernie Madoff
- Fraud
- Ponzi scheme

- $50 billion
- Life in prison
- Victims

Technically, Bernie is my mom's uncle, but he was always just referred to as "Uncle Bernie" growing up. We didn't have a close relationship, but I do remember going over to *one* of his houses in Palm Beach when I was a kid and being amazed that there was a full tree in his living room with a space in the roof where it grew through. Now, staring at that TV screen, it didn't matter how I was related to him. I was just in awe of the fact that I was connected to this person who could do something so awful.

I realized this was not just a financial slipup with some family drama. My great-uncle was the biggest financial fraud in the history of Wall Street, stealing more than $65 billion from a huge list of clients. On the outside he was the former chairman of Nasdaq and the founder of an investment company with clients like Steven Spielberg and Kevin Bacon. In reality he was running a Ponzi scheme, which means he was using investments from new investors to show unreal returns for old investors. He had been telling people on paper they had money that they didn't have for more than twenty years. Finally, investors' requests to redeem their money exceeded what Bernie had in the bank—which caused the moral mudslide of December 2008.

I told my parents I knew. I saw his face on the TV. We all sat down as a family and tried to process together, but it was almost impossible to absorb in that moment. Everything had changed.

BULLDOZED BY REALITY

How often do you see something big happening on the news or debated all over social media? I'm talking about stories of war, poverty, people falling ill with some rare disease, wildfires burning down whole towns, people losing loved ones in tragic ways, and so on.

I feel like I hear about those kinds of stories all the time. Maybe even every day.

But how often do those stories really change or impact the way we live? How often do they affect our everyday lives? If you're like me, not often.

I think the reason we're not affected is that most of us have a box in our brains that we use to store or process those events. That box has a label that says, "Things That Will Never Happen to Me—Move On!" Most of those huge items in the news are events that have never touched our palette of experience, so we don't even need to imagine what it would be like to experience it. So we stuff the story in our box and move on.

At some point, though, each of us gets hit with reality. In some cases, we're bulldozed by reality. We are touched by one of those huge experiences in a very real way, and it changes everything.

When reality hits us that way, it makes us realize that *anything* can happen. Anything. We're not immune from the big stuff.

That's a scary moment. And that's exactly what I experienced during the whole Bernie Madoff scandal. Suddenly one of those big news events was sitting right there in my living room, right there in my family. And the news headlines became my reality.

I still had a few more days before holiday break started, so I went to school the next morning and sat down in history class. Exams were over, so teachers were just filling time with whatever they wanted to. Mr. Brown walked into the classroom, turned on the projector, and my heart stopped.

Right there on the screen a picture of my uncle took up an entire wall.

"Does anyone know who this man is?" he asked, with a grin on his face. I think he was finally excited to be talking about current events rather than the same curriculum over and over. I was not as excited.

"Madoff! The guy who stole everyone's money!" a student shouted proudly.

"Very good!" Mr. Brown exclaimed, and the student sat taller in her chair.

I gripped the edges of my desk.

"But how could he steal so much money?" another student asked. "Did he have help? Did people know?"

"Some people in his office probably knew, and then he had his family who was in on it," Mr. Brown said with confidence like he was explaining that one plus one equals two.

Without raising my hand, I clapped back, "You don't know that."

I heard chairs moving as everyone in the class (or at least it felt like everyone) turned to look at me. It was like I had just told our history teacher that the Constitution isn't real.

"His whole family was reaping the benefits of his scheme," said Mr. Brown. "The houses, the yachts, the vacations. You're telling me you think they genuinely didn't know they were sitting beside a fraud at the dinner table?"

I wanted to be like: *One, I never went on their yachts. Two, our vacations were camping.* But that was beside the point, and it would blow my cover.

"Yes, that's what I'm saying," I said. "The family lost all of their money too. They were victims like everyone else." I could have gone on. I could have said that they also have to experience the betrayal of a family member and the chaos of the media, but I decided to stop there to avoid suspicion.

Mr. Brown asked me to stay after class and asked me why I was so passionate about this story. I told him I didn't think it was right to educate a class on his opinions and present them as facts. He agreed and appreciated my rebuttal. But he also seemed suspicious since I couldn't tell you the last five presidents but all of a sudden was passionate about current events.

I walked outside of class, and a girl I didn't know was waiting outside. "Are you guys victims?" she asked quietly.

I paused and looked around. It was only the two of us in the hallway.

"Yes," I said. "But don't tell anyone."

"Shoot—I'm sorry," she said. "That man is a monster."

I nodded my head and forced a smile. Then I went to the bathroom and cried.

KNOWING MAKES YOU STRONGER

Anything can happen. That's the lesson I learned from Uncle Bernie. And you know what? That's a lesson I *needed* to learn. Because anything really can happen at any moment, and it helps to be prepared.

As I said earlier, each of us gets hit with that reality at some point in our lives.

Here's what I've concluded after ten years of processing this whole situation: I'm fortunate that I learned the lesson of "anything can happen" at a relatively young age. Mind you, I'm not saying the crisis was good or that I'm glad my family had to go through such a terrible time. But I can look back and see that learning that particular lesson as a high schooler prepared me to embrace optimism when I encountered more anything-can-happen moments later in my life.

What I've come to realize is that the sooner we're confronted with the reality that anything can happen to us in life, the sooner we can start preparing for those moments. Better yet, the stronger we'll be when those moments come. If we accept the reality that anything can happen at any time, we won't waste as much time in our initial "what the heck just happened" stage and we'll be better armed and ready for what life has to throw at us.

Here's what else I've learned: accepting the truth that anything can happen gives us a higher level of understanding and compassion for the people in our lives who are currently experiencing those big moments. It gives us empathy. It helps us not be so quick to fill up our "Things That Will Never Happen to Me" box and move on.

That's what my family experienced as we learned those lessons together.

DEFINING "EVERYTHING"

A few years prior to the Bernie incident, my family had decided we wouldn't do Christmas gifts anymore; we'd just go to the beach and have family time. This is partly because my dad is really hard to buy gifts for and partly because we all wanted an excuse to go to the beach during winter. All the Bernie mess unfolded in early December, so that year our tickets and reservations were already booked to spend Christmas at Fort Myers Beach, and they were nonrefundable.

So we packed our bags and went to Fort Myers Beach. When we arrived, we went to the grocery and got all the food we'd need, including a bunch of frozen pizzas so we wouldn't have to go out to eat.

That first night in the hotel room, my dad said to my sister and me, "Your mom is kind of out of it with everything that has happened, so just do me a favor and don't let her do anything on this trip. Try to take the lead so she doesn't have to."

Seems reasonable, I know. But anyone who knows my mom can tell you that *was not* a reasonable request. Trying to get her to not work is basically like telling someone who does CrossFit not to talk about CrossFit. It doesn't work.

We were all sitting on the couch watching *Rudolph the Red-Nosed Reindeer*, but all of us were uneasy. We couldn't relax. We all felt off being there under those circumstances.

Then my sister sniffed the air and said, "It smells like something is burning."

We looked over, and the oven in the hotel room was blowing black smoke into the air. My mom and dad ran over, turned off the oven, and pulled out a black, rock-hard pizza with the cardboard still attached to the bottom.

"Oh, man—I forgot to take the cardboard off the pizza!" my mom said. "And then I forgot about the pizza entirely!"

My dad immediately shot a look at my sister and me while he was holding the burnt pizza. "Girls! I told you not to let your mother do anything!"

Everyone paused for a moment, and then we all broke into laughter. Not the polite laughter you give when someone makes an unsuccessful attempt at humor; this was on-the-floor, tears-streaming, and maybe-a-little-pee-just-came-out laughter. I'm not sure if it was the burnt pizza, my mom being a space cadet, my dad being mad at me and my sister for my mom burning pizza, or the fact that our lives were totally turned upside down in the most unpredictable way. Or maybe it was a combination of it all.

But no matter the cause, it was a moment we all needed.

That evening we were in the elevator going down to go walk on the beach when a man got on the elevator in the middle of our conversation. I don't quite remember what was said on our end, but it was something addressing the fact that all of our money was gone. You know, small elevator discussions.

The man who got on the elevator looked at us and said, "I lost my daughter two weeks ago in a car accident, and I'd give any amount of money to have her back."

As we walked on the beach, we walked in silence thinking about what that man had just said. Most of our money was gone, but our family was still here. We were all in this together, and we had each other. Throughout all of this, I could never say "we lost everything," because that wasn't the truth. We lost our *money*, but that's not even close to "everything." We had what we needed most: we had each other.

It sounds cliché, but I always thought of family as just something that would always be there. It's like Starbucks in Manhattan; you can turn any corner and there it is.

But this event made our relationship as a family different. We had never experienced anything that made us hold on to each other so tightly.

EXPERIENCE VS. STORY

The situation was the same across the board for my family, but everyone survived and coped in a different way. There was no recipe or guideline for how to bounce back from losing all of your money in a very public scandal that involved your family. (If there are guidelines for this, please send them my way.) But when you experience something you can't control, you will amaze yourself with what you can achieve when you have to.

Let's face it, there are a lot of things we can't control. We can't control if it's going to rain on our wedding day. We can't control if the Chinese takeout place gets our order right. We can't control the person who rear-ended our car when we were sitting at a red light. We can't control the crying baby on the plane. We can't control the sweaty dude who sat next to us on the bus. We can't control how many pink Starbursts will be in the pack. We can't control how much toilet paper our friends have in their house when we need it. We can't control our spouse, who refuses to watch *Titanic* purely out of pride. We can't control our neighbor's dog serenading the rest of the apartment building at 2:00 a.m.

I believe the moments in our lives that we can't control are classified as our *experiences*. They happen and life keeps moving. The curtain opened and closed, and now everyone has left the auditorium and the floors are being swept.

But our *stories* are how we interpret, internalize, and react to our experiences. We can experience being caught in the rain, but the story we tell about it could either be: I got drenched and it ruined my new boots and my day, or I decided to walk a little slower and just let the rain wash over me because life's not that serious.

If there is one thing that this experience with Bernie taught me, it's this: we can't control our experiences, but we can always write our stories.

Being related to Bernie Madoff and losing all our money was our experience, but it was far from our story. Now, almost ten years later, it's truly amazing to see how my family wrote different stories about the same experience.

Take my grandparents, for example. They had retired years ago and invested all of their retirement savings with Bernie. He was their brother-in-law and someone they had known for more than fifty years. Needless to say, when Bernie went under, my grandparents were hit with the terrible realization that every cent to their name was gone. Everything they were living off of for retirement and everything they had saved to pass on to their kids when they passed—all of it was gone.

They were in their seventies, so they weren't exactly in a prime position to start applying for jobs. My grandma and grandpa both realized that one of the things they could still do is drive cars. In fact, they both enjoyed driving to the point that, even though they previously had the means to fly, they usually chose to drive on trips instead. It was fun! So they registered their cars, got taxi permits, and started an airport ride service called Need-A-Ride. They put a magnet on the side of their car with their phone number on it, and they told all of their friends in the neighborhood to call them if they needed a ride to the airport.

The first job they took was New Year's Eve 2008, only twenty-three days after discovering they had lost everything. How's *that* for a quick start-up?

When I went to visit them a few months later, they were doing as many as thirteen rides a day to the airport. In their late seventies, they were using their iPhones to check flight times, leaving at 2:00 a.m. for pickups, and using Waze to get to the airports.

Over eight years they made 25,000 trips and traveled more than 1,300,000 miles.

Or consider my parents, who eventually sold everything they owned and have lived full-time in an RV for four years. And get this: they're now park rangers!

Boiling water can soften a potato but harden an egg. The same environment can produce two totally different results. Setting an early alarm can make one person feel super productive with those extra few hours but make another person feel cranky and robbed of sleep. This means the circumstance doesn't have as much influence as the subject. We are more powerful than anything that happens to us because our circumstances don't control us unless we let them.

Destiny is not an uncontrollable future; it's an active decision to write your own story. We are not what has happened to us. We are the story we write from it. We can write stories of fear or we can write stories of possibility.

THE POWER OF POSSIBILITY

Understanding that anything can happen in life is a key to embracing optimism. But in order for us to use that key, we need to recognize that it has two sides.

The first side to that key is *fear*—the fear of knowing that something bad can happen to us at any time. It's being aware that we're always at risk to pull the short end of the stick. Or that we can't control our universe, so instead we hide from it. When we get focused on the fear side of the key, we become so scared of what *might* happen that we quit before we even start. We think, *If I don't know what happens next, why even try?* The fear of the unknown takes us out of the game.

The second side of the "anything can happen" key is *possibility*. It's the acknowledgment that you could lose all your money tomorrow—*or* you might win the lottery. The idea that our lives will always have uncertainty means they also have possibility. The world can be our oyster.

When we recognize the power of possibility, we understand that nothing is a sure thing, so we must live loudly and do everything we love because the apocalypse could happen any minute. Or you could find out your uncle is a huge fraud. Either one.

You could pick up a guitar for the first time today and be on tour with Coldplay a year from now. You could start a business tomorrow that Apple acquires in three months. You could go on a blind date and meet the love of your life. You could try aerial yoga and get recruited by Cirque du Soleil.

A woman named Jennie McCormick dropped out of high school and served chicken-combo meals at a fast food joint, then she became the first amateur astronomer to discover a new planet since 1781. Another woman named Annie Duke studied cognitive linguistics in an Ivy League graduate program and went on to be a world-class poker player.[4] Your future can be drastically different from your present if you're open to possibilities. And that's what optimism is all about; instead of being paralyzed by uncertainty, you're energized by possibility.

Now, I'm not going to tell you that the day after the burnt pizza incident my family all popped out of bed and said, "Everything happens for a reason." We didn't. We sat in the pain for a long time before we started to become aware of the silver linings or began typing our new stories.

So even if you don't know what the silver lining is right now, that doesn't mean you won't discover it later. Some silver linings just take longer to develop, so it's okay to see a moment for what it is at that moment: a really tough situation. I'm not pressuring you to immediately see the good in everything because then I'd be pushing you to be borderline delusional, and your therapist would be mad at me.

When reality bites, get mad, feel sad, and be confused. Feel it all. Light something on fire in a controlled environment with buckets of water close by. You have full permission to feel whatever you want to feel in that moment without looking for the deeper lesson of what this all means. If we push away our feelings before we feel them, it's like pushing away your taxes. Eventually, the IRS will come get you and so will your emotions. Trust me, my accountant knows this stuff.

But don't stop there. Keep your eyes open for possibilities and opportunities. Because anything can happen. And when you are actively looking for possibilities and opportunities, you have a much better chance of finding them.

It wasn't until recently that I found the perfect analogy for these "anything can happen" moments. I was in Sequoia National Park with my family, and I was feeling sad when I saw all the burn marks from fires that had spread across the ground and scorched several acres of trees.

But then my sister (who is part my sister and part Bear Grylls) gave me a lesson: "The natural wildfires are actually good for the trees," she said. "Sequoia trees are dependent on fires to clear the path and release new seeds for growth."

That's exactly what happened with our family in 2008. The same fire that burned us also gave us a new life we had never planned. It opened up possibilities for me that I had never dreamed of before—and learning that anything can happen helped me see those opportunities when they finally came my way.

Take It or Leave It

Take a moment and write out the most ridiculous list of what your future could hold. Maybe you could train your dog to answer the phone. Maybe you could be the first female president. Maybe you could become an expert on fungi and give a TED Talk about it. Anything can happen, so dream of the possibilities.

LET THE *wonder* BE *bigger* THAN THE LIMITS.

#chasingthebrightside

Three

YES, AND . . .

Don't be intimidated by what you don't know.
That can be your greatest strength and ensure
that you do things differently than anyone else.
—SARA BLAKELY

The only times I've ever performed as part of a cast was when I was a tree in *A Charlie Brown Christmas* in middle school, and then again when I signed up for improv comedy classes thirteen years later. I had just started booking speaking engagements, and one of my friends said taking improv classes helped him be more relaxed onstage and more creative in his material.

So every Wednesday night for eight weeks, I drove forty-five minutes to a comedy theater and attempted to be witty and funny on command, like a nervous boyfriend meeting the parents for the first time.

I had no idea that improv was going to teach me a mind-set that would open so many doors. One of the golden rules of improv is a response called "yes, and . . ." When you're improvising with someone in a scene, they could say something like: "Hey, Jess. Do you see that big mountain of spaghetti off in the distance?" Then you have to acknowledge their improvisation as the truth by saying "yes" and justify it with your own truth built on top of that, which is the "and . . .": "*Yes*, Billy, I do see that mountain of spaghetti off in the distance, *and* we should go run through these pastures of risotto and cross the Alfredo lake to get to it."

Then, your partner would "yes, and . . ." to what you just said to continue to build the story. But imagine if the scene went like this:

Partner: "Hey, Jess, do you see that mountain of spaghetti off in the distance?"
Me: "No."
End scene.

Not exactly a story we'd tell at parties. When we say yes to something, it moves us from one place to the next. It takes us to the mountain of spaghetti and lets us ride down it on a meatball. But when we say no, we stay in the exact same room we're in right now. Saying no keeps the door shut, but saying yes leads to possibility—even when we don't know what that possibility is.

LET'S IMPROVISE

I think playing Monopoly as a kid skewed my perception of adulthood. Everyone starts with $1,500, and you can just buy a house. Monopoly should have credit cards where you keep spending money until you have to move back in with your parents. Now *that* would be a game I'd like to play.

But in Monopoly you have to roll the dice in order to move. And that's exactly how "yes, and . . ." works. To have a chance at winning (aka retiring and living in a mansion while all your other friends go bankrupt), you have to move forward on the board or else you go to jail. (Monopoly's rules, not mine.)

Saying yes is like the national anthem of optimism. When we say yes to an idea, an opportunity, a new relationship, or even a new item on a menu that we can't pronounce, we're expanding our palette of experiences. And when we expand our palette of experiences, we have more opportunities for stories and growth. We can't taste food we've never tried. We can't shake the hand of someone we've never met. And we certainly can't explore mountains of spaghetti.

In improv when you say no, you stand right where you are because you haven't built on top of your story. When you say no in life, you leave yourself with nothing to build because you've closed the door.

So even if we're not *exactly* sure what will happen when we say yes, we're at least opening the door to the potential of something good. And that's a core element of practicing optimism: being open to the possibility of good.

I used this "yes, and . . ." principle when I worked at Disney World as a college intern.

I'll be honest, I was never really a Disney kid growing up. Don't get me wrong, I loved watching Disney Channel movies with my sister, but I've met people with Tinker Bell tattooed on their ankle, people who can name all seven dwarves like the Pledge of Allegiance. On a scale of one to Neverland, I was probably a four.

But after I got to college, I was eager to get my feet wet with experience and start gaining professional skills, so I was intrigued when I saw a sign for the Disney College Program posted on a bulletin board at my dorm, a program where you work at Disney World for college credit.

Okay, I lied. I was going through one of those "first love" breakups with my high school boyfriend. You know, one of those early relationships where you start naming your future kids based on trivial moments of your past, like: "Let's name our first kid Hamlet, because that's the book we were reading when we met in class." When we broke up during the first semester of college, Disney World seemed like a good "start fresh" button for me. (I'm also really glad I don't have to name my firstborn Hamlet.)

I went to the information session that evening and heard from students who had just gotten back from the program and had experienced "the most magical time ever!" Either the program was really great or they had sipped too much Cinderella Kool-Aid. Either way, I was ready to take my chances.

I signed up and had a phone interview with a woman who asked me what I would do if a customer spilled their drink.

"I'd pour them a new drink."

Either my answer was not as obvious as I thought or she was just trying to meet her quota, because within a few days I was accepted to the program. They didn't give any details about where I'd be working or what I'd be doing, just that I was in the program and had to show up in a few weeks at Casting. (They call it Casting, not Hiring, because all their workers are "cast members," not employees, and because they're part of the Disney performance.)

Of course, my mom acted as if Walt Disney himself had personally invited me to work for him, but I still had to decide if I was going to pack my bags and take off for six months in a land far, far away. (Okay, Orlando, but still.)

FORGET THE "BUT"

In improv comedy, there are three ways you can move when it's your turn to talk:

- "Yes, and . . ."
- "No."
- "Yes, but . . ."

"Yes, but . . ." is where a lot of us live. We acknowledge a good idea or opportunity but talk ourselves out of it. The "but" is enough to shut the door and let someone else squeeze ahead of us and get the job we wanted or the relationship we daydreamed about. The "but" is easier to say than "no," but it is powerful enough to cancel the opportunity. You can be warm to the idea but not follow through, which can create the same outcome as saying no because you're staying in the same room.

For my decision about going to Disney, my "yes, but . . ." could have been:

- Yes, but I don't know anyone who will be there.
- Yes, but I don't deserve to go on this adventure while my family is still trying to get on their feet.
- Yes, but I know zero Disney trivia.
- Yes, but I don't speak four languages.
- Yes, but I don't even know what my job will be.
- Yes, but I might get behind on school credit.
- Yes, but where will I live?
- Yes, but what do I bring?
- Yes, but I don't really like Disney and what if I accidentally say that out loud and set off an alarm?

It's easy to dim our lights with one single "but." However, the "but" will always be there if you're looking for it. You can always find a reason *not* to take a risk. Just because we don't have all the information doesn't mean we shouldn't go for it, though. Right?

We can't let the fear of the unknown become bigger than the excitement of possibility.

"Yes, and . . ." triggers the expansiveness of what could happen, even if you don't know what those "happenings" are yet.

SELL IT

Improv is about convincing the audience of the truth you're building. If your partner says to you, "Today is the day! We're finally the chosen ones to visit this new planet called Banana Land," and your response is, "Yeah, whatever, I'd rather watch *The Office* reruns," that's not very convincing to the audience. They're not excited that you're going to Banana Land or that Banana Land even exists.

In the same regard, we can't "yeah, whatever" our own ideas and opportunities. We have to say, "Heck, yes! Let's make like a banana and split!" We have to use our enthusiasm to sell it to ourselves just as much as we'd sell it to an audience.

Do you remember walking through the mall—which was probably years ago, because, well, Amazon Prime—and there would be kiosks in the middle selling toys, hair straighteners, or dog leashes? There would be a sales rep posted beside it, ready to sell you on whatever the heck they were selling:

- "This toy is so cool that all of your friends will want to come to *your* house from now on."
- "Check out this hair straightener! It basically straightens your hair in your sleep!"
- "Man, this dog leash is the best. It changes color to reflect your dog's mood."

According to them, whatever they were selling was "the only thing you'd ever need." Any second of your life that ticked by without their product was wasted.

When we sell something, we have to be excited about it. We have to focus on the good features and make them stand out. These sales reps have to be so good at showing the best features that people will willingly stop what they're doing and listen. That's what we have to do when we sell something to ourselves: we have to amplify all of the great possibilities instead of brewing in the doubt.

Selling it to ourselves doesn't mean that we have to know the outcome or that everything has to go perfectly, because experiences in all forms (even the ones that don't go so well) are still valuable and carried with us the rest of our lives. And just think, one day I could tell my future kids that I was the real Mickey Mouse.

Side note: that didn't actually happen. Mickey had to be like five foot three and I'm five foot eight. I also have no coordination, so I wouldn't have been able to nail the parade dance.

Just like we'd try to convince an audience on an improv stage, we have to have that same excitement for our own "yes, and . . ." moments. In order for our optimistic beliefs to turn into actionable behaviors, we have to not just "yes" our ideas but "*heck*, yes!" our ideas. Get amped up for them as much as you got amped up when Netflix spent $100 million to renew *Friends*. Get so excited that you FaceTime your mom. Get so excited that you devote a page in your planner to this idea. Because if we say "yes, but . . ." or "maybe" to our ideas, we're actually closer to no than yes. Being more excited about the potential of good than the fear of the unknown is leading with optimism.

I said "yes, and . . ." to the idea of going to Disney World. I clicked the "accept" checkbox on the application, informed my roommate I would not be returning the next semester (side note: this "roommate" would become the future president of Headbands of Hope, and she still gives me crap about leaving her during our freshman year to go to Disney World), and I signed up for online classes through my advisor. I stuffed a suitcase full of professional workplace clothes (not realizing I'd be wearing a Disney costume every day) and drove ten hours to Disney World blasting the *Toy Story* soundtrack, which is still my favorite movie of all time.

I remember driving under the Welcome to Disney World arch and having a mix of childhood excitement that I was in Disney World coupled with a what-the-heck-am-I-doing-here attitude. I pulled up to Casting and waited in a long line of overly excited college students talking about, "If you could be *any* Disney character, which one would you be?!"

At that point, I felt out of place. I didn't know all the princesses and I certainly didn't hum "It's a Small World" in the shower while rubbing my armpits with a Mickey bar of soap. I also realized that a lot of people were there with groups from their school, so most people knew each other. I was the only one doing this program from my school, so I guess it was just going to be a ticket for one on the Tower of Terror.

WHAT DID I GET MYSELF INTO?

I want to take a minute to address this "oh, crap" feeling when I showed up because it's important. We talk so much about saying yes and going for it but then casually skip over the "oh, crap" feeling when you get there. Like when all of your friends are telling you to just go for it and get bangs and then the stylist spins you around and you're not sure if you look like Heidi Klum or Chewbacca. We can sell ourselves during the buildup, but it's a totally different experience when you're actually experiencing it.

So when you get that "oh, crap" feeling, it's natural to conclude in your head that you made a mistake and maybe you should have stayed home. But I'm here to tell you that if you feel that way when things start to roll forward, that means you're doing it *right*. Anything new is almost always scary and unsettling, but that doesn't mean it's not going to be great. Saying yes and showing up to something big and new will rarely feel like putting on a pair of slippers that make you feel all warm and cozy. It actually might make you feel like you left without your umbrella on a rainy day and you're wondering why you didn't just stay at home? But if the big leaps were easy, everyone would take them. So give yourself some grace. We need to give ourselves a buffer period when we say yes. If we're comfortable and confident, we probably didn't make that big of a move.

And one more thing: this "oh, crap" feeling will pass. It might pass like a Category 5 hurricane that takes out your power and drops an oak tree on your car. But it will pass. The clouds will part, and what was once new and scary will start to feel like home.

After waiting in line for a few hours and questioning my life as a whole and if I should get bangs, I finally got to the counter and gave them my name. They told me I was going to be working in the food and beverage service at the Main Street Bakery in the Magic Kingdom. I was beyond ecstatic. The Magic Kingdom was like the White House of Disney World, *and* I loved food! It was all coming together. Just like that the "oh, crap" feeling started to pass.

I worked in the Magic Kingdom at Main Street Bakery from January until May. Then I applied for an extension of my program over the summer and was transferred to work as a PhotoPass photographer. I had just as much photography experience as I did with baked goods—zero—but I was into it. Little did I know becoming a PhotoPass photographer was the job that would single-handedly change the course of my life. Imagine if I had said no because I had never worked a camera before?

Imagine if LeBron had said no to playing basketball because he never played before? Imagine if Kelly Clarkson had said no to *American Idol* because she'd never been on TV before? Imagine if Rachael Ray had said no to cooking because she'd never preheated an oven before?

Imagine if you said no to an opportunity that will change your life just because you haven't done it before.

SHOW UP

I didn't know it at the time, but my Disney experience was me using "yes, and . . ." to move to the next space on the Monopoly board . . . and the next . . . and the next . . . until you finally look back at your path in the game and realize that saying yes and rolling the dice was the smartest thing you could have done.

Saying yes and showing up is kind of like learning to ride a bike. You have no idea what you're doing, and your parents are hanging on to both sides of you as you try to push one pedal in front of the next. Before you know it, you look back and you didn't even realize you've been riding your bike by yourself for three blocks because you're so focused on staying upright and moving forward.

One day you'll look back and realize you're doing it. It may not feel like you have a handle on it, but you've been riding your bike for miles, and your parents are calling the local police because you don't know how to turn around and go back. (That's actually a true story from when I learned to ride a bike.)

A lot of narratives are told about opportunities that just happen to us magically, with no effort at all. To everyone who's ever told that story, I'm calling BS. If we sit and wait for something to work in our favor, that's the only thing that will happen: sitting and waiting.

There are not enough stories about opportunities that are created because we chased them. Going to Disney was me choosing to create an opportunity; I wasn't just magically placed there with pixie dust (although that would have been a really cool way to start the internship). Even when you aim to create opportunity and it doesn't work out, something may come of it that you didn't expect.

Experiences can't happen to us if we're not present for them. We'll never ride the best roller coaster if we don't wait in line. We'll never get the promotion if we don't show up to work. We'll never join the a cappella group if we don't show up to auditions. We'll never bake the confetti cake if we don't crack the first egg.

Showing up means nothing more than just being there. It doesn't mean you have to have an agenda or a grand plan; it just means you're ringing the doorbell and you're ready for what's next. When we give ourselves permission to just show up and nothing more, we're telling ourselves to just be there and see what happens.

Of all the things we use to weigh our opportunities, saying yes to showing up should be at the top of our list. What would happen if we just showed up and that's it? No pressure to network or get financial gain; just show up. Buy the ticket. Reserve your seat. Open the door and be there.

Optimism is about spending more time going down the path of yes than no. What could happen? What's possible from this? What would it look like if it all worked out? When we "yes, and . . ." our own lives, we're coming from an open-minded place. And I'd rather have my mind open with possibility than closed with a rigid belief.

Walking into an improv scene, there's no script. Having no script can be scary and you can feel small and unprepared, or it can be an opportunity to become whatever you want. A lot of times we look for signs of resistance so we can create the "but" or the "no" and stay in our comfort zone where we know the Wi-Fi password. But in improv, you *have* to look for ways to build. You have to paint murals of possibility onto walls of doubt. You have to say "yes, and . . ." to create opportunity now, at this very moment.

Yes, I'll go to Disney World . . .

- and I might meet amazing people.
- and I might work for an awesome company.
- and I might learn new skills.
- and I might just use this experience to start a company that helps hundreds of thousands of kids all over the world.

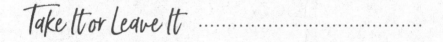

Take It or Leave It

When you're weighing an opportunity, toy with some improv. Explore saying "yes" to what's in front of you, and then make a list of "ands" that could come from it.

HARD TIMES ARE EITHER THE *excuse* TO DO LESS OR THE *reason* TO DO MORE.

#chasingthebrightside

Four

IF IT ISN'T THERE, CREATE IT

If you don't see a clear path for what you want,
sometimes you have to make it for yourself.
—MINDY KALING

I came up with the idea to start my company, Headbands of Hope, when I was in college. When it came to me, I was not struck by a lightning bolt of brilliance. I cannot look back and say, "That was it! Eureka! Yahtzee!" Much to my disappointment, the clouds didn't part, the birds didn't start chirping, and voices in my head didn't exalt me to elation.

No, I stumbled into my business idea as a sort of knee-jerk reaction to solve a problem, like putting tape around a leaky pipe. And the more I've asked around, the more I've realized that most of us have discovered we're on the right path only after we've passed thirty Cracker Barrels and have been driving awhile. We had to learn to swim after we got in the pool. We did not experience a lightning bolt of inspiration from the sky. We were just opening and walking through doors from room to room: optimistic, hopeful, and willing to leap.

My idea grew out of a problem, and that problem, believe it or not, was wigs. Yes, you read that correctly.

When I was working in Disney World as a PhotoPass photographer,

I got to photograph people from all around the world enjoying the parks and trying to forget how much money they spent to be there. But my favorite moments to photograph were kids who were there on a trip with the Make-A-Wish Foundation, an organization that grants wishes to kids with life-threatening illnesses. Going to Disney World is one of their most popular wishes, so I got to meet a lot of families and photograph them meeting the princesses or seeing the castle for the first time. They were some of the most moving moments I've ever experienced, and I was blown away by the impact this organization could have on these kids and their families.

When I got home from my Disney internship, I applied for an internship with the Make-A-Wish Foundation in Charlotte, North Carolina, for the summer before my junior year. Actually, they didn't have internships set up yet, but I called their offices and persuaded them to meet with me. I told them about my experience at Disney World and the kids I got to meet and how I wanted to help. I told them I would happily do *anything* they didn't want to do. They accepted my offer and agreed to let me show up to the office every day during the week. They reimbursed my parking and opened my heart even bigger to the cause of encouraging children who were sick.

When I was working there, I wasn't doing glamorous things. I was cold-calling people to donate and getting hung up on most of the time. I was organizing their supply closets, stuffing envelopes, and doing anything they'd let me do.

On paper, my "internship" at Make-A-Wish didn't look like the most glamorous gig, but it didn't matter to me. I was *so happy* to be there. Every single thing I did, I could connect to making a wish come true. It didn't matter what I was doing because all my work had meaning, no matter what.

My favorite thing was meeting with the families to figure out what their child wanted as his or her wish. We'd get tons of pictures sent to the office of kids receiving their wishes, and I loved sorting through them and adding them to the wall where we posted pictures from all of the wish trips. One trend I noticed was how so many of the kids would wear headbands after losing their hair to chemotherapy. Almost every picture of a girl included a fun, colorful headband, and they looked adorable.

"What do the hospitals do when the kids lose their hair?" I asked in the office.

"Usually there are wigs and hats given out," they replied.

I thought, *Why would they only give out wigs and hats when they're wearing headbands?*

I thought about it some more, and I just *loved* what the message of wearing a headband meant to these kids. They weren't hiding the fact that they had cancer with a wig; they were embracing their journeys while restoring their self-confidence with a simple accessory.

To them, a headband was their sense of normalcy. It was a reminder that, no matter what, they're still beautiful. I loved that.

FILLING THE GAPS

Let's pause here for a moment. I'll admit this connection of headbands and kids with cancer was the *spark* of my idea. This was like realizing when your feet are cold, you can put a blanket on them. It wasn't a moment of genius, it was a recognition of *need*.

To me, entrepreneurship seems so fancy. And intimidating. Like investors, equity, funding, accelerator, *blah blah blah*. For a while, I didn't even know what a lot of those words meant. (And for some of them, now, I still just smile and nod.) But I've realized that, at its core, entrepreneurship is just about creating what you want to see in the world. In other words, entrepreneurship is like filling a gap.

When we fill the gap, we're providing value. When a hose is leaking, you find something to cover the leak. When you're hungry, you eat. When it rains, you get an umbrella. When your jeans rip, you sew them (or pretend it's fashion). When you're low on gas, you fill up your tank. When something is missing or needed, you fill it.

I spoke at an event a while ago with Marc Randolph, cofounder of Netflix. He classifies entrepreneurship as "looking for pain." In theory, looking for pain sounds weird and morbid, but businesses can only operate if they're providing value. And the best way to provide value is by fulfilling a need and solving a problem, whatever that problem may be. Problems aren't necessarily life or death. We have social problems, like how it's hard to meet people when you move to a new city. Or functional problems, like how hard it is to poach an egg. (Am I the only one who can't do it?)

Solving problems doesn't have to mean starting a business. When I wanted an internship at Make-A-Wish and they didn't have one, I created it. When you wish something was there and it isn't, you learn the value of it instead of just trying to create something out of thin air.

Do you wish there was a dog park closer to you? Write a letter to your city council. Do you wish there was a local Facebook group to bring together artists in the community? Create it. Chances are, if it's something you want, other people will see the value in it too.

BE THE GOOD

Toward the end of my internship, I met a four-year-old girl named Renee who had a brain tumor. Her wish was to go to Disney World to meet Sleeping Beauty. They let me be more involved in this wish since I had proven I could handle it. Shortly before her trip, she went to the doctor and had a scan on her tumor. The result was not what they were hoping for. Renee had rejected all the treatments they had tried, and her tumor had only grown. She was too sick to go on her wish, so the trip was cancelled.

When I heard the news about her condition, it was as if someone had switched off a light in the room. How could this happen? I knew how excited she was for her trip and how badly she wanted to meet Sleeping Beauty. She *deserved* to have her wish.

With the help of the Make-A-Wish team after work that day, I rented a Sleeping Beauty costume and arrived at her house. I brought her a matching dress and a crown that had her name on it. My time as a photographer in Disney World was paying off as I tried to mimic all of the princesses I had photographed. I spent the afternoon with Renee and her family, read her the story of *Sleeping Beauty* (all the while in character), and tried my best to make her wish come true.

As I looked around the room, I saw all of her family's eyes on Renee. All of their eyes had tears of joy as they watched her gaze at Sleeping Beauty. I remember reading the book in my best princess voice and trying not to cry. This moment was for her, which meant my feelings and emotions needed to wait.

I blew her and her family a kiss goodbye as I left. When I got home, I walked straight to my room, pulled the door shut, and cried.

Optimism isn't about being happy all the time. It's not about avoiding situations to stay in your happy place. It's about being willing to be exposed to the bad in order to see the good. Otherwise, if we don't put ourselves in those shoes, we'd never know how to help.

Sitting there crying in my room, I was totally stripped of everything I thought was important. Everything I had worried about an hour ago suddenly seemed so trivial. I had trouble navigating my feelings because it was such a sad moment to be a part of, but I was able to provide some *good* in it. And that good was something her mom reminded me of when she called me a few weeks later to tell me Renee had passed away.

"She got everything she ever wanted: to meet Sleeping Beauty," her mom said.

And even though her mom and her family were clearly in pain that I can't even begin to fathom, they saw the good in the moment: Renee got her wish. She spent an afternoon with Sleeping Beauty.

That led me to think, *What if I could provide that "good" to other families like this in my own way?*

THE EXCUSE OR THE REASON

I realized that a tough moment like I had with Renee could trigger two things:

1. A hard time could be an *excuse* to do less and retreat. Why would I put myself in a situation where I could experience pain like this again?
2. A hard time could be a *reason* to do more and step forward. Since I've seen this firsthand, what can I do to help in the future?

Hard times are either the excuse to do less or the reason to do more. The choice is ours.

Excuses are born out of fear. When we want to remove ourselves from discomfort, we look for a way to do that. *This is too hard. I'm not ready yet.*

But reasons to move forward are born out of optimism. We can take a negative experience and use it as a propeller to create change instead of building a wall and calling it a day. So instead of "This is too hard," we say "Even though this is hard, it's still necessary."

The moment with Renee was both difficult and powerful, but I had to choose what story I'd write from this experience.

SURVEY YOUR PAIN

Ideas and inspiration aren't always born out of a swanky co-working space with latte machines. Sometimes, like Marc Randolph said, they're born in pain. But optimism is not about ignoring the pain and bouncing to a happy place; it's about surveying it. It might sound weird to "survey" your pain or someone else's, but when we ask questions around it, we understand what's wrong and what needs to change. How does this happen? What could help? What could I do? What needs to be different to prevent this or make it better?

When we ask ourselves these questions, we're not just sitting in pain, we're changing it. Notice how "Why me?" isn't on that list of questions. "Why me?" shifts the focus to our ego, not the problem at hand. And "Why me?" will always seek the excuse to do less, not the reason to do more.

I couldn't just let this be a fleeting time in my life that led to nothing. Renee had to be the heartbeat to something wonderful. But what?

Headbands.

The small trend I had noticed connecting headbands to kids with cancer started to sizzle on the frying pan a bit more. So naturally I headed to the computer in my dorm room and asked my good friend Google.

I typed: *Giving headbands to kids with cancer.*

My search results included small crafting events where attendees made headbands for kids with cancer; it was nothing major. More results came up when I typed *sweet potatoes with faces on them*, which was a surprisingly common search and I highly recommend it.

I was heading into my junior year of college. My major was communications with a minor in Spanish. Basically I was taking anything *but* entrepreneurship classes (one of my classes included Rock Climbing 101). I still have to use spell-check to spell *entrepreneur.*

I remember that moment in time, sitting at that computer, like it was yesterday. For some reason, out of all the moments in my life, this is one of the clearest. All my searches trying to find someone somewhere who was giving headbands to kids with cancer were coming up dry. It wasn't happening.

Why not me? I thought.

It wasn't a moment of clarity triggering a brilliant business idea; it was more a calming feeling of optimism. *This is a problem, and I'm going to be the one to solve it.*

The first time I said it out loud was at a hibachi restaurant with my family. Because what better way to announce a life goal than over that delicious white shrimp sauce? I said to them, "I have this idea to start a company that gives headbands to kids with cancer. I've decided I'm not going to study abroad and I'm going to stay here and work on my idea."

"That's wonderful," they said. And then I stabbed my chicken with a single chopstick to bring it to my mouth and started dreaming of what this headband thing was going to look like.

IT'S YOUR TURN

If big and wonderful endeavors can be born out of a short moment in our lives, that means we have to be ready when they come. We can't miss the idea because we're too worried about whether or not we're ready.

So why not you? Why can't you be the one to solve the problem? I know, this question is super cheesy, but I've said this to myself on *many* occasions, usually right before I'm about to do something scary like give a big speech or pay my taxes. We can be optimistic about a solution to a problem, but do we believe that we can be the ones to fix it?

Everyone who's ever done something great has always had to believe that they could be the one to do it. Everyone who's ever solved a problem was once just pondering an idea. But everyone who's done something great had to have a moment where they turned that idea into action.

Forget how much money you have (or don't have), or where you went to school, how old you are, or what you scored on your SAT (I *bombed* that thing). Replace all of those limiting beliefs you have about yourself with possibility.

- I'm too young or old. Are there other people my age I could team up with for this?

- ~~I'm too inexperienced.~~ Do I know anyone who could give me some pointers?
- ~~I don't know enough people.~~ Are there any networking groups in my area?
- ~~I've never started a business before.~~ What online resources are available to first-time entrepreneurs?
- ~~I don't have enough time.~~ Could I get up an hour earlier every day to work on this idea?

LET THE WONDER BE BIGGER THAN THE LIMITS

All right, I'll admit it, ideas can be scary. Why? Because ideas mean something new. And *new* means uncharted territory. And uncharted territory doesn't come with a clear guide, and we don't know what kind of *National Geographic* animals are living out there. The fear of limits is natural when it comes to ideas, but whether or not we let limits become an excuse is up to us.

The biggest barrier to success is not what you know or your experience level. The biggest barrier to success is the belief that someone else is more capable or suitable to lead, solve, create, organize, or (fill in the blank) than you. The barrier is the belief that someone else will take care of this idea, not you.

Role-play with me for a second. No commitments, no business plans, no big life changes. Just come sit in a place of optimism for three minutes.

What if you were the one to make the world better?
Where would you start?
What ideas do you see?
What would you do right now to breathe some life into it?

When we can take our minds on a journey of what could go right, we let optimism do its job. Because inspiration is the result of optimism. When we envision a better world, we're inspired to create it.

Optimism starts with little sparks of idea or vision, but it's up to us to decide whether we're going to follow them through. I didn't know how I was going to do it, but I knew this idea was going to be my contribution to the world. I was going to give headbands to kids with cancer.

I opened up my spiral notebook and wrote *Headbands* at the top, and the adventure began.

Take It or Leave It ·····································

List out all the things you're frustrated by or wish were different, whether it's a long carpool line or kids without access to education. What could you do to change them for the better?

JUST BECAUSE YOU HEAR crickets DOESN'T MEAN NO ONE IS listening.

Five

BABY STEPS

You can, you should, and if you're
brave enough to start, you will.
—STEPHEN KING

When I first discovered that kids with cancer like to wear headbands, I thought maybe I could buy them in bulk and ship them to hospitals. Except that required money, and I was eating ramen noodles and waiting weeks to do laundry so I wouldn't have to pay the two dollars to use the machines.

Not happening.

Next thought: What if I could find companies that make headbands and convince them to donate the extras they're not using, and I'll coordinate distribution? There we go.

So I hit up Google and typed: *Large corporations that make headbands.*

Goody hair accessories popped up at the top. I clicked to their website and found a contact button with an 800 number. I whipped out my sparkly Razr flip phone (don't you miss flip phones?) and dialed.

After pressing option keys for about five minutes, I finally made it to: *For all other inquiries, press 9.*

Operator: Goody hair accessories, how can I direct your call?

Me: Well . . . I'm not sure. I have this idea, and I'm wondering
if you guys will work with me on this. I've noticed that a
bunch of kids are losing their hair to chemotherapy and
they are only being offered wigs and hats, but a lot of
them enjoy wearing headbands. Maybe you guys could
donate your extra inventory to children's hospitals? I'll help
arrange the whole thing! Oh—my name is Jess, by the way.

She forwarded me to another person who went straight to voicemail.
I recited the same speech and waited anxiously for a callback. Days later
it still didn't come. So like any sane person would do, I set an alarm to
call the Goody info line every day between my Spanish and Lit classes,
at 11:00 a.m. I'd say something along the lines of, "Hello there! It's Jess
calling about headband donations again. I'd love to discuss the opportunity to donate headbands to children's hospitals. Please call me back at
your earliest convenience."

I added in "earliest convenience" on the third call or so, because I
thought it made me sound more professional.

Two weeks and fifteen calls later, I got a call back.

Goody Person: Hi Jess, this is Goody hair accessories calling
about a headband donation. We really appreciate your
persistence. How many headbands do you need?

Here's what was going through my head: *(1) Holy cow, they called me
back! (2) Why haven't I thought of how many headbands I need?*

Me: Let's do a thousand to start.

A thousand seemed like a *huge* number to my nineteen-year-old self.
But surprisingly, they agreed without skipping a beat.

One week later, a thousand headbands showed up in boxes to my dorm room.

My roommate thought I was crazy, but I went to hospitals and events and handed out the headbands, and the kids *loved* them. The looks on their faces solidified that this was a good idea. The parents were so grateful, and the hospital staff kept saying what a breath of fresh air headbands were as opposed to wigs and hats. At that point, I knew I was on to something.

After I was all out of headbands, I came to the hard truth that I couldn't keep waiting on Goody to call me back to do this. I needed to come up with something that could consistently give headbands to kids with cancer without relying on a callback.

A few months before my Make-A-Wish internship, Blake Mycoskie, founder of TOMS shoes, was the homecoming speaker at my university, NC State. His business model was that for every pair of shoes sold, they'd donate a pair of shoes to a child in need. Blake talked about how he wants his business to be an example of how other companies can use their One for One® model to make a difference, which I thought was super cool. You don't see many businesses giving away ideas and encouraging other people to use them!

Thinking about the TOMS One for One model, I thought maybe I could use that to give headbands to kids with cancer.

After a few crumpled sheets of paper, here was the idea: I'd sell headbands, and for every headband I'd sell, I'd donate a headband to a child with cancer.

I called it Headbands of Hope.

So here I was, sitting in my dorm room with this idea to start a headband company that gives back to kids with cancer. It felt like I was just told to make Thanksgiving dinner for the whole neighborhood and I had never used an oven before. But the gravy was simmering, and I was not about to let the neighborhood down.

BREAK THE SEAL

Looking at an idea in its entirety can be daunting. And quite frankly, when you think of *everything* you have to do and *all* the things that have to go right, you'll probably talk yourself out of it. I know I've done that a time or two!

But sometimes all we need to do is break the seal to show that we're totally qualified and it's not so scary. By breaking the seal, I mean just *starting*, even if it's something super small like telling someone about it or doing a simple Google search to see what's out there. When we sit with ideas in our heads, they brew and brew into a giant cloud of doubt, and we start questioning ourselves so much that we become paralyzed with fear.

Small actions give us the confidence to do bigger actions later on. Have you ever put something small on your to-do list, like unloading the dishwasher, and then you do it and it feels really good to cross it off your list? Then maybe you start wiping the counters and you turn on your speakers and before you know it, you're KonMari-ing your entire closet.

Even the idea of writing this book was daunting. I told myself to just write a few paragraphs and see how it felt. Then I wrote an outline. Then I wrote a chapter. Then I started telling people I was writing a book. And now here we are having wonderful people like you read it!

But if I didn't tell myself to *just* write a few paragraphs, I may have never written an entire book.

Think of the daunting dream that's ahead of you, then decide something small you can do right now to break the seal. Don't think about the long path ahead, just one small thing you can do today.

For me, I started by telling all of my professors what I was doing and asked if I could use my business as classwork for my communications courses. Instead of creating a media kit for a random company for the assignment, I'd create it for my own. Most of them agreed to let me do it. Even when we had to have an internship during our senior year, I put together a presentation for my professor pitching the idea that I intern for myself so I could work on my business. Surprisingly, he agreed as long as I had supervision, which my public relations professor at the time, Dr. Maria De Moya, graciously agreed to do.

But I still knew *nothing* about starting a business. I knew more about cloud formations and Spanish pronouns than I did about business. So I pulled out my university directory and looked up the business department and started searching for professors who had experience in consumer products or retail—or who were just smiling in their headshots and looked like they might say yes to talking to me. I reached out and requested fifteen minutes of their time to ask them questions.

Here were some of my questions:

- Do you have a template I can use for a business plan? Also, what's a business plan?
- What are taxes, and should I care about them?
- If you were me with this idea, what are the first three things you would do?
- Know anyone with money?
- Let's be honest, how far do you think I could get based on personality alone?
- What pitfalls do you usually see young entrepreneurs fall into?
- When would be the right time to apply for *Shark Tank*?

I got tons of great feedback from professors and now had a clear to-do list:

- Get a trademark.
- Register my business with the state.
- Open a bank account.
- Make a website.
- Create the product.
- Make a logo.

- Get business cards.
- Start social media handles.
- Get a Kardashian to wear my headbands.

Okay, so the last one didn't happen until years later. (Thanks, Khloé!)

But as I started forming my to-do list, I decided I would just tackle what I could in that moment. When my friends were out doing stuff, I'd post up in the library where the computers had bigger monitors and work on my business for hours. With each task I checked off, I was getting closer and closer to my dream and further and further away from the fear of beginning. Each thing I did, no matter how small, was breaking the seal of fear.

WHAT'S RIGHT IN FRONT OF YOU?

I never thought about raising money or getting investors early on because I didn't know how that worked. Eventually I did have to ask for money, and it didn't turn out so well (more on that later).

But at the time, I decided to focus on what was right in front of me. I may not have had a lot of money or a lot of business experience, but I was on a college campus, so what could that do for me?

I went over to the graphic design school and introduced myself to the teacher (I wasn't in her class). I told her what I was working on and asked if she could make it a class assignment to make me a logo, and I'd pick the best one and give that person headbands (even though I didn't have headbands yet).

She agreed. And *that's* how I got my first logo.

Then I needed to build a website. Small problem, I barely knew how to operate Microsoft Word. I found where the computer design classes were and what times they were meeting. I wasn't allowed inside the class (because I wasn't a registered student *in* the class), so I stood outside the room when the class let out and asked random students if they'd teach me how to build a website for my business idea.

One girl agreed to help me because she liked the idea of Headbands of Hope. For weeks I met with her in the computer design library every day for lunch, and I "paid" her in Chipotle burritos to teach me how to build my website. One burrito equaled one hour of learning Shopify and Photoshop. I'd like to take a moment to thank the people at Chipotle for making my business possible . . . and the girl who accepted burritos as payment.

I also didn't have the money to buy a nice camera, and this was before iPhones made everyone look like professional photographers. The library at my university had technology rentals, so I would rent a nice camera from the library to take product photos on a white poster board I bought from CVS. If there was a wait list for the camera, I'd beg the librarian to let me use it for an hour and I'd give her a headband.

Along with product photos, I needed "people photos" for the website. We now call these lifestyle photos, but back then I just knew them as *people* photos. I've evolved.

I decided to rent a camera from the library and try to take pictures of people wearing headbands myself since I couldn't afford to hire a photographer. I found a spot in a park and sent out a Facebook event calling for models (or anyone who would show up and put a headband on and let me take their picture). For some reason I thought people wouldn't show up, so I did what you do to ensure people will show up: provide food.

I'm not sure what possessed me to do what came next, but I thought it was a brilliant idea that maybe Jimmy John's would want to sponsor my photo shoot. I went in and asked the manager if they'd be willing to donate sandwiches for the models to eat so I could get "people photos," and shockingly they said yes.

My Facebook event listing said something like: "I'm looking to get pictures of people wearing Headbands of Hope! Come to Moore Square Park this Saturday at 4:00 p.m., and I'll take your picture in a headband. Oh, and there will be *free sandwiches from Jimmy John's!*"

I showed up with the bare essentials for a photo shoot: a camera, headbands, and a trunk full of Turkey Tom sandwiches. Twenty people showed up, and I got a bunch of amateur photos to use for the website because I don't know how to use a camera. Because obviously my time at Disney didn't pay off.

Moral of the story: when in doubt, always provide sandwiches.

Second moral of the story: Jimmy John's is awesome.

Little by little, pieces of my business idea started to come together by just focusing on what I had, not on what I didn't. In fact, one of the main pieces of advice I give to start-ups is look at what's right in front of you instead of looking over the fence at what your neighbor has or where you think you should be at this stage.

A lot of people ask me how I started a business in college because the stigma is that school is a barrier to business and you have to drop out in order to fully pursue your dreams. But college was my low-hanging fruit. It was what was right in front of me. I turned it into a springboard for my business, not a brick wall I had to overcome. Most times when I see businesses fail, it's not because of a lack of resources; it's because of a lack of being resourceful.

It's okay if you don't have an email list of thousands of subscribers. Maybe you're in a community Facebook group where you can post about your business. It's okay if you don't have a warehouse with a fulfillment team shipping out orders. Maybe you invite some friends over and open a bottle (or a box) of pinot grigio and pack orders while watching *Bridesmaids*.

Look at what you have in this very moment, and start there.

BABY STEPS ARE STILL STEPS

Before I knew a lot about digital marketing or Facebook ads (who am I kidding, I still have no idea how to create Facebook ads), I came up with what I thought was a brilliant marketing tactic: print hundreds of flyers about Headbands of Hope, go to every Starbucks in a one-hundred-mile radius, and post the flyers on their bulletin boards.

I would also bring flyers with me when I traveled so I could slap them on Starbucks bulletin boards wherever I went. Innovative, I know. [Brushes off shoulders.]

To this day, I don't think anyone has seen Headbands of Hope and been like, "Oh, yes! This is the company I discovered on that flyer at Starbucks."

Who knows? Maybe one person did see a flyer and followed us on social media. And if that's the case, that's great. Because baby steps are still steps. I was learning to walk and that's okay. Give yourself some grace when it comes to hitting the ground running. You're going to make mistakes, and you're going to look back and laugh at some of the things you thought were a good use of your time.

At times you might feel like you're speaking into a microphone in front of all these people, and you keep tapping it, and you ask, "Is this thing on?" The world is chaotic, and sometimes it takes a little bit for you to find your audience. But don't let that stop you from taking one step at a time. Just because you hear crickets doesn't mean no one is listening.

Let's face it, the success you have pictured might not be exactly how the story goes, but never dismiss yourself out of the gate. Either way, action puts you on a totally different playing field than being removed and stagnant. You are now a problem-solver, a contributor, a difference-maker, and you're in this club of people who went for it. You've graduated into a group of go-getters that just might lead to other opportunities you never even thought of before. But in order to be in the club, you have to take the first step. And then another.

Before you know it, your baby steps will lead to firsts. I remember where I was standing when I got my first order on the website from someone I didn't know. I remember the first time someone wrote an article about me. I remember the first time someone asked me to speak about my story. I remember the first time I saw my product "in the wild" on someone's head (it was at an airport).

No matter how small, a step is a step, and each one means forward progress.

So let me ask you this: What feels light for you right now?

Start with what feels easiest and what you're most excited to do. Maybe that's sketching out your idea for how it would look. Maybe it's doing a bit of research. Maybe it's asking to meet with someone who's walked a similar path.

Don't think about all the mountains you have to climb. Just go fill up your water bottle. Then pack your bag. Get in the car and drive there.

Baby steps are still steps. When we don't burden ourselves with the heaviness of a long to-do list, it makes everything seem more manageable. Because it is. You can handle it.

And if I could handle all the crazy things I was about to do, I could handle anything.

Take It or Leave It ·······································

Make a list of all the resources you have right in front of you that could help you get where you want to go. Know anyone who can help? Any free resources online that would be helpful? Are there any groups or meetups with like-minded people you could join? What can you do right now with little effort to make that first step?

DON'T
LET YOUR
plans
KILL YOUR
possibilities.

Six

SHE MADE IT WORK

And I knew exactly what to do. But in a much
more real sense, I had no idea what to do.
—MICHAEL SCOTT, *THE OFFICE*

Recently I was talking to one of my friends, Adrian France, who cofounded a very successful digital company called Odyssey, and we were laughing about all the crazy things we had done to get started creating our companies.

She joked, "If you never ran around your house and took every piece of technology you have to a pawn shop in order to meet payroll for your employees the next day, then you don't know my life."

But she was serious. She actually did that.

The thing is, that's how *most* big things start: in a state of messy panic where you're just throwing darts and you probably accidentally left your hair straightener on this morning. If this is you, welcome to the club! Happy you're here. Now go turn your straightener off before you read the rest of this chapter.

If this isn't you, and instead you're waiting until you have the perfect plan or more *professional* experience or you need to have your apartment white-glove clean with all of your hangers facing the same direction, dishes done, and mail filed away in colorfully tabbed folders, then allow me to show you an alternative approach to pursuing your ideas. Just walk with me for a second.

I'm going to ask you to wander away from your safely organized, alphabetical, color-coded folder of ideas because we develop in the *process*, not in the *planning*.

I like to call this beginning phase of chaotic goal pursuing, "She Made It Work."

The She Made It Work stories are my favorite because it's what makes us real. Those are the stories that show our hearts, because we were willing to jump for something we believe in, even when we're fully aware it might not be a soft landing. The She Made It Work moments are what separate the optimists from the pessimists, because you have to believe there will be good in order to push your limits. If the end result is something extrinsic, like money or status, your grit and courage won't be strong enough. But if you truly believe in the meaning of the end result, a lot of things that seem crazy to others actually make perfect sense to you.

Because the crazy is always worth it if it works.

When people ask how I started my business, it's easy to go to the nuts and bolts: well, I made a plan, built a support system, and worked really hard for it every day. But that answer isn't serving anyone because you can find that answer in any Q&A interview from any entrepreneur. It's like seeing firework pictures on your Facebook news feed on the Fourth of July.

Fireworks on the Fourth of July? Groundbreaking.

There are crazy things I've done in pursuit of my dreams that seemed like good ideas at the time. Some of them worked, a lot of them didn't, but I'm proud of them all. It's all a part of my story. There are the stories we tell on social media that we twist to paint this perfect picture where all worked out. Where we ride peacefully into the sunset on horseback and everyone watching on social media is like, *Man, she has it all figured out.*

But I like hearing the stories where that horse gets stung by a wasp and you're holding on for dear life yelling, "Down, Bessy! Down!" Not because

I like seeing people panic, but because the tough times are where we're built. I can learn more from someone who was at the bottom and had to work their way up than someone telling me how clear the air is at the top. So I like hearing stories that tell the narrative of grit, not the pretty picture.

I'll be honest, when I was first starting out I fell into the spell that we had to only share our successes and be perfect all the time. I would smile and rattle off all of our recent success and wait for others to *ooh* and *ahh*. But all that was giving me was a feeling of exhaustion, because I was tired of pretending to be someone I wasn't. Even more, I felt isolated because I felt like I was the only one experiencing these hurdles.

When I started being more transparent, I became proud of my ups and downs. And when I started to be more transparent, more people started to be transparent with me. People whom I had known for years were telling me stories that I had never heard before. When we can own our failures or crazy moments, it gives people around us the freedom to do the same.

I want to tell you some of these stories to show that sometimes optimism requires trial and error. We're not going to get it right on the first try, and we will definitely look back on some of the things we did and say to ourselves, *Really? What was I thinking?!*

But these stories are necessary for us to find our way. And when you let your optimism guide you, you're so focused on your good vision that a lot of these crazy stories seem worth it.

So let's kick off our shoes, wiggle our toes staring back at us with three-week-old nail polish, and hear some of the crazy (and borderline stupid) stuff I've done to get my business idea off the ground!

SHE MADE IT WORK #1

I signed up to be a vendor at a music festival the summer after I started Headbands of Hope. This was a big deal because I had never done an event I had to travel to (it was in Delaware, and I was in North Carolina), and it was a few thousand dollars to be a vendor. That was a pretty big fee for me at the time. But they had reached out to us and said they were picking a few select vendors they thought would be a good fit since it was their first year doing the music festival, and they wanted to keep the vendors curated.

My mind went to people dancing outside to the Lumineers and wearing our flower crowns. I was all in. I paid the fee and my then-roommate Lauren, who's now my right-hand woman at Headbands of Hope, knew someone we could crash with in Delaware to save money on lodging.

About three weeks before the event, I reached out to see what time we should be there, move-in instructions, hours of the event, and all the basic details. No response. I emailed again, and still no response. I went onto their website, and they didn't have a phone number or contact section. I started to get nervous that there wasn't even a festival at all. One day before I was supposed to leave, I still hadn't heard from anyone, and I had a meltdown in my car in the parking lot of a Walmart where I was buying displays for an event I wasn't even sure was happening.

The next day, we packed up the car with headbands and displays and drove eight hours to an event that may or may not have existed. Luckily we found the address to the event on Facebook, and when we showed up there were stages being set up. I breathed a sigh of relief that this was actually a thing. I got out of the car and asked any staff I could find where the vendors were supposed to go. No one knew what I was talking about.

Way across the field, I saw a tent with a table underneath it near a stage. I met eyes with Lauren and motioned over to the tent in the distance. We had no idea what the tent was for, but we had just driven eight hours and paid a few thousand dollars to be there, so that tent very well could have said Welcome Home. It was mine.

It had started to lightly mist, so we wanted to move quickly. We couldn't drive on the grass, so we opened up the car and piled boxes in our hands and started trekking across the field. About a quarter of the way there, a downpour started. Every step we took, we got muddier and muddier. It was literally our version of a Tough Mudder race. It took us around five trips to the car and back to move all of our stuff over to the tent that we claimed without asking.

We set up, did the festival, and sold around $6,000 worth of headbands in just a few days. No one said anything about the tent, and we drove back muddy, smelly, and smiling.

This was one of the first encounters I had where I realized that some people will let you down. You can tattoo the contract on your forearm, and some people will still not hold up their end of the deal. But sometimes you can just show up like you own the place and move as if everyone is on your side. When you act as if you're doing what you're supposed to be doing, people will start to believe you.

SHE MADE IT WORK #2

Despite my photography stint at Disney World, my skills weren't really translating into good pictures for the website. However, I couldn't afford to hire a photographer for a shoot. Instead, I found photographers (real ones) and asked if I could ship them headbands to use for their shoots. I discovered a lot of photographers pay for their own props and styles for shoots, so if I could provide some for free in exchange for using the photos, it could be a win-win.

I shipped boxes of headbands out to dozens of photographers, and that was how I got my first professional "people" photos.

Now, almost 100 percent of our content on Headbands of Hope is user generated. People tag us wearing their headbands, and we repost. What better "models" than the people who actually wear us?

SHE MADE IT WORK #3

Around the time when *The Bachelor* and *The Bachelorette* series were really hot—who am I kidding? I still watch those shows—I realized that people who were on the show had a lot of followers on social media, but they weren't huge celebrities who were impossible to get in touch with.

So I started emailing, commenting, and sliding into the DMs of reality-show stars. Surprisingly, quite a few said yes to wearing our product and posting to their followers. (You might not find love on *The Bachelor*, but you might get something better: a headband from me.)

I realized giving away free product to people with large followings was a small price to pay for the exposure we would receive.

SHE MADE IT WORK #4

One of our first big breaks was getting a story on the *Today Show*. They called and wanted to do a story on the mission of Headbands of Hope and myself as an entrepreneur.

Have you read between the lines that I'm always quick to be agreeable? Well, that happened again.

On the phone, they asked if they could do some filming at the hospital with me passing out headbands, and then in my office where I work. "Yes, of course!" I said. We nailed down the date they'd fly in, and I hung up.

One small problem: I was still working out of the closest Starbucks or at my kitchen table. I didn't have an office yet.

I found a co-working space called HQ Raleigh and told them the situation. Then I asked if I could use one of their offices temporarily, so I could shoot for the *Today Show*. Fortunately, they were on board.

I went to Staples and got a logo printed and slapped it on the wall of "my" 12 x 12 office suite. I stacked some headband displays on the side tables, put up some pictures, set up my computer, and ordered a coffee mug with my logo on it from Vistaprint, rush ship. I'm not sure why I thought the coffee mug with the logo would be the finishing touch of "my office." But I still love that mug.

They came and filmed, and the story was beautiful. I watched it on my couch with my friends in our pj's eating breakfast biscuits from Bojangles'.

If a good opportunity knocks, say yes and then figure it out after.

SHE MADE IT WORK #5

One time a local women's boutique placed an order for headbands. I realized that this store had one hundred other locations, but each was independently owned. So I got the list of locations and called every single other store and told them about Headbands of Hope. I told them other stores were starting to carry them (okay it was a *store*, singular, not *stores*).

After one hundred phone calls, three coffees, and one day of my life, I received zero orders.

About a month later, that entire boutique chain declared bankruptcy, and they shut down all locations.

Hey, sometimes you fish in a lake and realize there are no fish. It happens.

SHE MADE IT WORK #6

Through some hard-core Googling, I found the name of an agent for a really popular female athlete. From there, naturally, I did some internet stalking and found the agent's email. I wrote him a letter about how grateful I'd be if this athlete would wear my headband. I also saw on his website that he was located in Los Angeles, so I added that I'd love to meet him next time I was in the LA area.

Surprisingly, he wrote back and said he'd run it by her, and he said he'd love to meet me next time I was in LA. Here's how I read the email: *She's definitely going to wear the headband and you should fly to LA.*

If there's one thing I've learned about relationships, it's that things move a zillion times faster in person than over email or phone. There have been many times when I've lied about "being in the area for XYZ reason" when really I'm just ready to hop on a plane if they'll meet with me. I know it's crazy, but it can work and it has worked for me in big ways. Except this time, it didn't.

I told him that "coincidentally" I'd be in LA in the coming weeks and asked if he was free. He said yes, we nailed down a time and date, and he gave me his office address. I bought a ticket to LA and landed to an email on my phone asking to reschedule for next time.

So, I went to In-N-Out to make my trip worthwhile. The burger was worth it.

Meeting the right people can do more for you than any business tip you might read. Never regret taking a risk to get in front of someone.

SHE MADE IT WORK #7

I was at an Avett Brothers concert and I had read the story of one of the band members, Bob Crawford, whose daughter had cancer. I went up to the edge of the stage during a break and handed them hats we had made and a gift bag of headbands for his daughter. They were so gracious and actually wore the hats for the second half of the concert!

Then a few months later we were doing our first promo video and we needed a song for the background. I loved the Avett Brothers song "At the Beach" and wanted to use it. I found the name of their manager and then found him on Twitter. I tweeted at him saying that I was the person at their concert in Charlotte who gave Bob the headbands for his daughter and hats for the band. Then I asked what it would take to use one of their songs for our upcoming promo video. He tweeted me back saying, "Let's talk." Then he direct messaged me his email.

They agreed to donate their song to us, and the video came out amazing. Thank you to the Avett Brothers—and also to Twitter.

Sometimes a shot in the dark can work, so don't stop trying.

SHE MADE IT WORK #8

When I interned in New York City for a summer a few months after I started Headbands of Hope, I'd walk down the streets with a box of headbands on my days off. I'd pop into any store that seemed promising and ask to speak with their buyer, then quickly launch into my pitch.

Though I really did not have much success going door-to-door, it quickly made my skin grow thicker so I could put myself out there more.

SHE MADE IT WORK #9

A few years into my business, I'd saved enough money to attend a big trade show in New York where stores from around the world came and picked products to put in their shops. The booth was $8,000, so it was definitely a gamble. I wanted to save money in every way possible, so I fit all the things I needed for the booth in two large checked bags instead of shipping them. Both bags were just under the fifty-pound weight limit, thank goodness.

When I arrived in New York, cabs were too expensive, so I decided to take the subway. I had taken the subway before, so that wasn't the issue. The issue was that some of the stations had stairs but no elevators or escalators (or not that I could find).

I remember standing at the bottom of a long flight of stairs, looking up and seeing the skyscrapers of New York City, and thinking to myself, *You can do this.*

I had my backpack on and put the suitcases at my sides. I took a deep breath, lifted both suitcases up, and ran up the flight of stairs like I was in the CrossFit Games. People were dodging me left and right because I was not stopping until I could smell the hotdog stand on the corner. I made it to the top, then walked ten blocks to the Javits Center and made a profit of $3,000 at my first show.

Sometimes the adrenaline fueled by optimism can make you muscle just about anything.

SHE MADE IT WORK #10

One time I was in the running for a grant from Kevin Plank, founder of Under Armour. I made it to the top five applicants, and then we had to pitch our ideas on a live broadcast stream. Spoiler alert: I didn't win the grant. Not only did I not win, but it was broadcast to all my friends, family, and Headbands of Hope fans who were tuning in to watch.

When they asked what I was going to do with the grant money, I said I wanted to host a prom at a children's hospital and create DIY headband kits for the patients to design and create their own headbands within the hospitals.

After I was rejected in the competition, I wallowed for about 28.5 hours, and then I decided I was going to find a way to fund those projects myself. So I did.

If you let it, rejection can give you the tenacity to find another way to accomplish your goals. When you use post-rejection tenacity to move forward, you'll eventually become so consumed in your work that you forget who you were trying to prove wrong anyway. (Because I've clearly forgotten all about Kevin Plank. Kevin who?)

I hope these stories about my humble beginnings prove that you don't have to have your first meeting in a skyscraper with a personal secretary. You can have it at the local coffee shop around the corner or on your living room floor with a pint of Ben & Jerry's Half Baked ice cream. Starting small or scrappy doesn't mean it's not working.

LET YOUR PASSION DO THE WORK

Do you remember your first crush? Do you remember the crazy things you did to get that person to notice you? My first crush was Harrison, my third-grade classmate. Harrison went swimming with dolphins for a family vacation, so I rented a book from the library about dolphins and wore dolphin earrings until he sparked the conversation.

Harrison: Do you have a pencil I can borrow?
Me: Dolphins can hold their breath for eight to ten minutes.

Needless to say, Harrison and I didn't work out. But being passionate about something can make you do crazy things, which drives innovation.

There's a window when our passion is at its peak. There's a moment in time when we're so excited about an idea or a goal that our mind starts racing with possibility. When we sit and wait too long, the internal dialogue starts to turn into *but what if* and *maybe that won't work* and *I'm too busy.*

So when you start to feel the crazy passion creeping in, run with it, because those are some of the most productive and creative hours you'll ever have.

Passion is the original 5-Hour ENERGY shot. So toss it back and let it do its job.

WINS ARE WINS

Like I mentioned earlier, my interview on the *Today Show* was one of our first big breaks, but I don't mean that exactly how it sounds. It was our first big break to the public eye, but it didn't catapult us into the wildly successful tier where Oprah returns my phone calls and everything got easy. In fact, there hasn't been any *one* thing that has done that for us. Looking back, we're successful because of all the tiny victories along the way. No matter how small the win, it's a step forward.

In the beginning of my business, all the wins (even the smallest of wins) felt like trophies for my mantel. We literally started from the bottom, so any step up was the difference between standing on the ground and floating. But then, as we grew and got bigger, my focus shifted to the "bigger wins" and I stopped celebrating the small ones. Then one day I realized I wasn't having that much fun anymore, and I realized it was because I stopped recognizing the wins. *Always* celebrate your wins, no matter if it's your first order from a friend or a purchase order from Target. A win is a win.

As part of my daily journaling, I write down wins, even the smallest ones, like going to bed early and getting a good night's sleep or not falling on my face in yoga class. Give yourself a pat on the back and you'll be more encouraged to do it again.

DON'T LET YOUR PLANS KILL YOUR POSSIBILITIES

I *love* hearing She Made It Work stories from other people because it shows their grit and optimism for endless possibilities. I never planned on running up to the stage at an Avett Brothers concert and eventually asking for the rights to use their song, but I'm so glad I did. At the end of the day, our plans are just educated guesses. It's fine and dandy to have a loose map of where you want to go, but don't be so rigid that you drive right by the World's Largest Ball of Twine in Cawker City, Kansas (it's 19,873 pounds).

Don't let your plans kill your possibilities just for the sake of sticking to the map.

When I put a destination into my GPS (I call her Bertha), she tells me the most efficient way to get there with the least amount of traffic, not taking into consideration what might happen that nobody can predict. But sometimes there is new construction going on or a family of turtles are crossing the road (that would be so cute). So you just take the closest exit and hope that Bertha redirects you another way. Thanks, Bertha!

My point is, just because there's a way that seems easy doesn't mean it's the *only* way; just because someone else has gone that way before does not mean it's the best path toward *your* goal. You might try it and it doesn't work, but that doesn't mean your journey is over. In fact, when you try a new way, you might discover something that wasn't on your road map before.

Although my path was all over the place, all of it was necessary to make me who I am today. I wanted to share with you some stories about the beginning of Headbands of Hope because, now, those days are pretty entertaining. I've come to terms with some stuff that happened then, and the sting is not so fresh.

Optimism is not all hearts and flowers. Optimism doesn't mean your great ideas will start working immediately. You might catch yourself sitting on your floor, hand-writing addresses on one hundred packages. But that's where optimism kicks in, knowing that everything is just pushing you forward to what's next. So you keep going.

Being relentless toward your dreams is not just a good thing, it's a necessity.

It was especially a necessity for when I messed up so bad that I almost quit before I even began.

Take It or Leave It

The next time your mind starts racing with ideas, act on one, even if it's small. Use your window of passion to execute on things you might talk yourself out of later.

FAILURE WILL *always* FEEL *better* THAN REGRET.

#chasingthebrightside

Seven

THROW A FAIL MARY

Because getting the wind knocked out of
you is the only way to remind your lungs
how much they like the taste of air.
—SARAH KAY

There may have been one *tiny* detail I left out when I was starting my business. As I was going down my "launch my business" checklist, the last thing I had to do was to get the actual headbands made. It was a task I had been putting off since I didn't even know where to begin with product manufacturing.

One professor pointed me to a website where you can search for manufacturers. I logged on and started sorting through thousands of entries, trying to find one that worked with elastic. Because if they made elastic, they could probably make headbands. That was the grand plan.

I reached out to hundreds of manufacturers that had "elastic" in their bios. I'd share a little about my idea and that I was looking for a manufacturer to make headbands. I had no idea of the "lingo" I was supposed to use: MOQ, product specs, samples, and so on. My .edu college email address probably didn't help my cause either. Even though I knew I didn't have it all figured out and that probably came across in my emails and calls, I was hoping someone would see the good and potential in what I was doing and take a chance on me.

Finally, after hundreds of failed attempts, one manufacturer in Kansas emailed me back, and I did a little happy dance at my computer.

We hopped on a call and I told her my idea, but I admitted I didn't know what I was doing and I was still in college. She told me not to worry and that she loved my idea and wanted to help me. I called my dad, who is also an entrepreneur, and told him I had found a manufacturer who was willing to guide me through the process. He was so excited for me and asked if I wanted him on any of the calls. I told him she was shipping me some samples and I'd let him know when I needed him.

I was so blindly excited to get up and running, I honestly didn't even look closely at the samples. In hindsight, they looked awful. The kids I babysat for could probably make better headbands. But they were headbands and I wanted to get moving, so I pretended like they were made with Swarovski crystals or something and told her they looked fabulous. I was ready to place an order.

She told me that the kind of material we were using was very hard to source, so we'd need to do a high volume. She sent me an invoice for a starting order . . .

It was $10,000.

Ten thousand dollars is a lot of money, even now. But at the time, $10,000 was like money you'd win on *Survivor* or a down payment for a house that's walking distance from a Whole Foods.

SPEAK UP

In hindsight, it's not that I didn't know I'd have to eventually pay for headbands, but I didn't want to bring it up because I didn't want to kill the vibe. I know that sounds ridiculous and it absolutely is. But I think it's important to address this messed-up perception I had about the situation.

I felt like because I was the smaller entity in this partnership, I should feel lucky that they were taking my calls. I didn't want to question them, even though I had every right to vet them as much as I thought they were vetting me.

When we're kids, we're taught to respect adults and not talk back. At this stage in my life, I hadn't fully transitioned into a place where I could question someone older or more experienced than me. I was so worried about being respectful and likeable that I wasn't listening to my gut.

Speaking up changes the dynamic of partnerships. The whole thing felt a little off to me, but I was so set on making this work that I didn't speak up. Sometimes when we're in a new space, we feel like everyone else around us are the experts and are not to be questioned. Some people go the extra mile to make you feel that way and let you know that *they* are in the driver's seat. But if something feels off, speak it. When you're confused, ask questions. When we use our voice, not only are we getting clarity on the situation at hand, we're also showing that we're not just going to sit quietly on the bench and let things slide.

———

I had no idea what manufacturing typically costs, so I didn't know what to expect. But I knew I didn't have that kind of money. Not even close.

I asked my dad with his business background to help walk me through this. My dad and I got on the phone with her, and she explained that the first purchase would be big because she needed to get all the materials. The rest would be smaller. We hung up the phone and I asked my dad what I should do.

Should I try to get an investor and give away a portion of my business in exchange for cash? Or should I get a loan from the bank and pay interest until I can pay it off?

My dad thought about it and the next day we had a meeting. He explained that giving away a portion of my company so early wasn't a good idea, and he didn't want me to have to get a loan and pay interest. Then he told me something I'd never forget.

"Jess, I really believe in your idea. I think this could be something big that could help so many people. I'll front you the $10,000, and you can pay me back when the business starts to make money."

Telling me that he was going to loan me $10,000 was like hearing my dog speak English. I couldn't believe it. My dad is a super giving and generous person. I've seen him do things for his employees and for random strangers that make me think if people were more like him, then the world wouldn't have any problems. But growing up, my parents were very good about not just *giving* us anything. Any gifts were earned and deserved. We were very fortunate to live in a nice neighborhood and go to really good schools, but nothing was ever extravagant or just handed to us.

I even remember going to other kids' birthday parties where they'd rent out the bowling alley and each kid in attendance got a new Barbie as a "parting gift." That's not how we did birthdays in my house. I remember when the show *Survivor* was all the rage. I had a *Survivor*-themed birthday party where we had to run around and pick up sticks in the yard while my mom timed us. Then we had to eat canned sardines as a "challenge." It was *awesome*. But needless to say, they didn't just toss around money, so my dad offering $10K to front my business was unfathomable.

Plus, my family was still recovering from losing their money, so this was not an easy thing for him and my mom to do by any means.

But to be honest, I didn't think twice about saying yes. I was so eager to just move forward, I immediately accepted his offer.

I gave him a huge hug and thanked him over and over again. "I promise I'll pay you back," I said.

I remember it was a Friday afternoon, and I ran to the bank with my dad to wire her the money because I wanted the factory to get it before the weekend. I walked into Wells Fargo with her banking information and printed instructions on how to wire money. I signed the papers and left with a smile on my face.

I followed up with her on Monday and she confirmed she received payment and would start production.

And that was the last time I ever heard from her.

Yes, you read that correctly. That was the last time I ever heard from her.

DEAD END OR U-TURN

After I realized the money was gone, I was physically sick to my stomach with guilt. My head was in the toilet, which is actually a normal place to be in a college dorm communal bathroom. I *wished* I was sick from drinking too much. But it was from dreaming too much. I had an ambition hangover. I felt like I went too far, and this was the consequence.

How could I be so stupid? Not only did I fail at my business, I had lost $10,000 of my dad's money that was hard to come by. My dad tried to get it back through lawyers, but she was gone. He never blamed me for what happened, but I blamed myself. I couldn't even look him in the eye whenever we talked about it.

I didn't tell any of my friends or my teachers what happened. I hoped that everyone would forget about this silly little idea and I could just fade into the background. If anything, I felt that this moment made it official that I wasn't cut out for this. I wasn't experienced enough, and now I had no money.

Frankly, my first inclination was to pretend like this never happened, like when you bomb the SATs and you tell people you haven't taken them yet. Not a ton of people knew about it, so it would be easy to sweep it under the rug. I would just get a job and pay my dad back as soon as I could. But when I went to bed that night, and every time I'd close my eyes, I couldn't stop thinking about all the kids I saw wearing headbands. I *still* saw the good, despite living in the bad. I couldn't turn off the possibilities.

And this is where optimism really kicks in, when you're up the creek without a paddle but you are *still* thinking about how great it would be to get to your destination.

Failure has the unique ability to look like two things: a dead end or a U-turn.

When we reach the end of a road, we have a choice: stop the car and call it a day or whip it around and try another way. But dead ends and U-turns can look exactly the same; it's up to us which way we turn the wheel.

WHAT FAILURE REALLY MEANS

I definitely didn't have this clarity at the time, but now I can confidently say that failure is not the opposite of success; it's a part of it. In fact, it's a rite of passage. I've met so many successful people, from Olympic athletes to musicians, entrepreneurs, and CEOs, and they *all* have a story like this.

In fact, it was millionaire entrepreneur Barbara Corcoran who said, "All my best successes came on the heels of failure."[5]

When Van Gogh was alive, he sold only one of his paintings . . . to a friend for not a lot of money. Bill Gates dropped out of Harvard to start a business that flopped. Lady Gaga was dropped from her first big record label. And Thomas Edison was secretly conducting an experiment at Western Union when he dropped some acid (like, literally spilled some acid) and it ate through the floor. See, we've all been there. We're human.

And I'd just like to be recognized for *not* saying that Michael Jordan was cut from his high school basketball team because, *We know, Michael. We know.*

So I'm sorry to be blunt, but if you've never encountered an "oh, crap" moment, that doesn't make you successful, it makes you safe. And how many people have we read about in our history books that created change when they were safe?

None.

Safety is great on boats, roller coasters, tiger exhibits, and highways, but not in ambition.

We don't become successful by avoiding failures; we become successful when we're strong enough to navigate them. When you try to do something big and put yourself out there, you're more prone to hiccups and speed bumps because you're taking risks and navigating new territory. This is reality, and we are going to have to get used to the vulnerability that comes with leaping. Some of your risk taking will work out great and some of it won't, but you'll never have those answers unless you go for it.

The more you get comfortable with reaching, the more comfortable you'll be hearing no. In the beginning, I felt all the nos *deeply*. Every no was like a bee sting, and I'm allergic to bees. But then you realize life goes on, everything keeps moving, and you choose to find another way or not.

JUST FOR TODAY

Saying that it was "just for today" made it easier to get motivated than telling myself to jump back on the horse, risk it all again, and never look back. I would ask myself these kinds of questions:

- What if just for today I went and looked up smaller manufacturers with lower minimum orders?
- What if just for today I met with the entrepreneurship department and asked for advice?
- What if just for today I go to Michaels and sew headbands by hand just to see how they look?

To answer the last question for you right now: they looked bad. Very bad.

But the point is, I made the next step smaller. Instead of telling myself to go run a marathon, I got myself out of bed each day and walked on the treadmill. I also gave myself the comfort of being able to stop tomorrow, which I never did.

I still remind myself of the option to quit at any moment and do something else. Most of what you read says something along the lines of "Quitting Is for Losers," which is usually printed on a poster of a lion chasing its prey or a snow-capped mountain with a guy hanging on with his pinkie. But that's not my take on it. I don't want to feel trapped in what I'm doing because we always have choices. I want to work toward something I *want* to do rather than work toward something I feel like I *have* to do. And if that feeling changes, I'll pass the baton and do something else.

Telling yourself you can quit at any moment isn't a reminder of weakness; it's a reminder of choice. And when we choose to keep going, we're choosing to recommit to our purpose.

Giving myself the option to just try again today and permission to stop tomorrow if I wanted was easier to rationalize than getting back into it full speed, all in. It was easier to just dip my toes in the water, then my feet, then my ankles, then my legs, and walk through the shallow end rather than jump off the diving board and belly flop back into this idea.

Optimism encourages us to dream big. But when we're dreaming big with optimism, it doesn't necessarily mean we have to *do* big at every moment. Treat yourself kindly and take things day by day. If we get mad at ourselves with every mistake or put too much heaviness on *everything* we do, we'll get burnt out and not do it at all. So what if "just for today" you did what feels light to you?

A few days after the incident, I submitted an application to the school treasury for a $300 grant they gave to students starting businesses. Within a few weeks, I received the grant, opened up a business bank account, and found a woman making headbands on Etsy. I asked if I could buy some from her. I started off with two styles of headbands with the $300 grant.

Those two styles grew into more than 250 products on our site today.

Whenever I experience failure now, I ask myself these questions:

- *What the heck?* Because sometimes you just need to say that out loud to understand what actually happened.
- *What can I learn from this?* In my $10K scenario, I learned that contracts and 30 percent deposits are my new best friends.
- *Who can I talk to about this?* Our failures become bullies when they sit in our heads and aren't spoken.
- *What do I have right now?* Look at what's in your control, not what you've lost.

And *sometimes*, I ask myself:

- *What's funny about this?* Because when all else fails, hopefully something was at least funny, so you can laugh about it or tell it at parties later on.

DON'T FALL FOR THE SHOW

One of the reasons I felt so alone during this failure was because I didn't hear any stories like mine. Everyone else seemed to be doing just fine. Have you ever met someone who's been successful and listened to them share "their story"? It usually goes something like this:

"One day I was making my morning avocado toast and realized there had to be a better way to get the avocado out of its shell and onto my toast. So just like that, I invented the avocado slicer. Now, I've revolution-ized the world of avocado lovers everywhere, making it easy for ordinary people to make exemplary avocado toast, guacamole, and dressings like never before. Chef Gordon Ramsay doesn't know what he would do with-out my handy-dandy avocado slicer."

How many times have you heard someone present their success story like this, as though they stumbled into a meaningful invention or career without scraping their knees and tripping a time or two or ten? We don't show each other our sweat stains or our face-plants. We don't broadcast the rebukes when we've been rightly criticized for a mistake. We don't share our failed experiments when we've launched a product nobody bought or when we nose-dived in ignorance. The fact is, most successful people only show their highlight reels, leaving the rest of us thinking the road to innovation is far easier than it is.

Let me tell you, if someone else's story is only perfect, they're hiding what lies beneath.

We all have front-row seats to the Happy Show on social media. In fact, if I scroll through my feed right now, I guarantee I can find the following:

- Another promotion!
- Another engagement!
- Another perfect newborn that doesn't cry!
- Another successful start-up!
- Another morning yoga session!
- Another romantic night out!
- Another perfectly balanced dinner!
- Another #TransformationTuesday with an epic weight loss!
- Another perfectly trained dog that has never peed inside!

If we (including me) were more honest on social media, it would probably be:

- I'm bloated from my takeout dinner last night.
- I'm not sure if my business is working, but I hope it is.
- I don't think my boss likes me.
- How the heck do you work a juicer?
- Another Tinder date that already made my palms sweaty.
- I only walk on the treadmill to watch a movie.
- I took this picture at a party and then went home immediately after.
- Rover just ate my Scrabble game and is now pooping out letters.

Of course I love to share and celebrate the good. But when that's all we're exposed to, it makes us feel like our mistakes or bad days are the exception in a sea full of double taps and likes. But when you're taking action and doing something big, the mistakes aren't the exception; they're the rule.

I have an online course called Mic Drop Workshop that helps women become professional speakers. The other day, I meant to post in the Mic Drop closed Facebook group about a gig I had coming up. The post said this: "Hey guys! I have a gig coming up on Wednesday that I'm trying out new material for and I'm feeling all the nerves. Just want to remind you that no matter how many times you do this, we're all human!"

When I went to check my Facebook the next day, I had all these notifications. When I clicked on it, I realized that I accidentally posted that on my personal page (with thousands of followers) instead of in the closed Mic Drop Workshop group.

I had all these people in the comments cheering me on and thanking me for my transparency. I got emails from people asking if I wanted to practice my new material with them before the gig. I even saw a notification from Facebook that said this was my highest-performing post!

It was something that I would have *never* thought to share publicly because it was vulnerable for me. But that mistake showed me how beautiful transparency and sharing our imperfections can be.

When was the last time you messed up? Five minutes ago? Great. Tell someone. Let's normalize the bumpy roads by changing the conversation around success. I feel like our success stories can be just as scripted as the Pledge of Allegiance: moment of inspiration leads to idea, which leads to success.

But the real script is: moment of inspiration that leads to an idea, OUCH, *WHACK*, OOPS, some success, *WHAM*, some more success, CRAP, and then sometimes feeling successful, sometimes thinking *why the heck am I here*. And then you keep going.

As soon as that voice in your head tells you you've failed simply because you made a mistake, silence it and remind yourself: you are blazing a new trail. Because with every dream, there is challenge. But with every challenge, there's change.

YOU ARE NOT YOUR MISTAKES

For a period after the $10,000 was stolen, I felt so alone. I made that failure a part of my identity rather than the great work I was trying to do. For a short time even after the $300 grant, that failure solidified all the voices in my head saying that I wasn't good enough and I was too inexperienced.

Years into my business, I began to receive invitations to speak at events about how Headbands of Hope got started. I was afraid if I told the *real* story of how I got started, they'd think I was not credible to speak publicly—until I received an invitation to speak to a small class for my former teacher, who wasn't able to teach that night. I showed up that evening tired from the day, and I stood there looking at a room of students who were in the exact same seat I was in a few years back. (Literally the same seat. I was in this class.) There were no adults to impress. These students didn't care if I was business-y, and I frankly couldn't muster up a talk-show personality to tell them a joyful (not fully true) story of inspiration and success.

So I did something I hadn't done before onstage. I told them the *whole* story.

And it was the most powerful speech I had given thus far.

It took me a good three years and some change to realize that this part of my story isn't what makes me unqualified; it's what makes me purposefully resilient. It wasn't my success that was helping students; it was my navigation of my failures. Now in my speeches I even share stories of other amazing people who have failure stories like mine. Even my dad told me stories he ran into with his business years ago, and I'd had no idea.

Who we are is not what happens to us but how we respond. You are not your mistakes. You don't have to walk around with a scarlet letter or feel like you have a skeleton in your closet. Failures are not indications of self-worth or your experience level. They're merely cuts and bruises that show you've walked through a thick forest.

And sometimes our greatest lessons come from our worst moments.

YOU JUST GET STRONGER

Failures are kind of like getting tackled in football (my husband played Division I football, so trust me, I know this stuff). The first time it happens, you're like, "What the heck just happened to me? Which way is up? Can I call my mom?"

But then the tackles become a normal part of the game. Some hurt more; some hurt less. Some are harder to get up from and some might give you a concussion so bad that you start ordering a Happy Meal in Mandarin.

But here's the cool part: the more you play, the more you understand the game. You can make more informed decisions, you can run plays that you know will work, you build a team, and your intuition becomes stronger. It doesn't mean you stop getting hit; you just get better at it and are quicker to get back on your feet.

That first hit is always the worst, but then it makes everything else that follows not seem so bad.

Since that $10K moment:

- Our warehouse was struck by lightning—twice.
- I've hired and fired friends.
- I spilled coffee all over myself on the way to deliver a keynote address.
- Our package to Gigi Hadid got lost, so she didn't wear our headband at Coachella.

- I ordered eight thousand of the wrong hang tags.
- I spent my savings on a trade show but a snowstorm hit, so no buyers showed up.
- I was on *Good Morning America* talking to Michael Strahan and my mic didn't work.

And much more has happened. But remember, these moments of struggle are not the *opposite* of success, they're a *part* of it. A successful path is not about the absence of resistance but the navigation of it.

GET BACK UP

One interception can't keep us from throwing another pass. If that was the case, there would be no more quarterbacks in the NFL and it would just be a really weird game of grown men playing keep-away. (Remember, I'm basically Nick Saban since my husband played football. You have to trust me when I use football analogies.)

In football the last-ditch effort for a team that's behind is to throw the ball really far into the end zone and pray that one of their players catches it. The play is called a Hail Mary. Well I've gotten pretty good at throwing Fail Marys, as I like to call them. To me, a Fail Mary is a big leap you take to attempt something that would be *worth* failing for. You can justify in your head that you'd rather fail at something big with the slight chance that it could work, than be comfortable staying right where you are.

Make the big ask for the promotion you deserve. Hop on that last-minute flight to try to get that meeting. Plan the date before you ask him or her out. Book the venue before you've sold the tickets. Register for Open Mic Night before you've written your comedy act. Preheat the oven before knowing the recipe.

Put yourself a mile ahead from where you're at now, and you'll be surprised how quickly you might get there.

FAILURE OVER REGRET

Let me be clear: optimism requires risk. And sometimes risk requires failure. And failing is hard. I'm not going to sugarcoat it. We can have conferences, books, and TED Talks about why failing is a good thing, but it doesn't make you pop confetti when you lose $10,000 of your dad's money. It's unfair to expect to be *so* comfortable with failing that you become immune to the emotional toll it takes on you. It's also unfair to expect that failures should be celebrated, because they're *hard*. I'm not trying to make failure seem light, but I am trying to tell you that even though it's hard, it's normal and necessary.

But if it hurts, why put yourself in the situation to be tackled? Because it's that much sweeter when you see the end zone right in front of you and you know you're about to do something great.

Failure will *always* feel better than regret.

Once you realize there is life after mistakes, you gain an untouchable level of confidence. My company now does millions of dollars in sales, and our headbands are carried in thousands of stores around the world. More importantly, we've donated headbands to every children's hospital in America and dozens of countries. But none of that would have ever happened if I turned away when that money was stolen. And I would never want your story to stop because of one bad pass.

P.S. Don't worry, I paid my dad back.

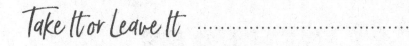

Next time you mess up, don't make it a secret. Tell someone. Make a joke out of it. Heck, you could be like me and make it a part of your speech. When failures sit in our heads, they become bigger than they actually are. When we speak them, we're not only changing the dialogue around failure, we're freeing ourselves from keeping an unnecessary secret.

SOMETIMES THE MAIN DIFFERENCE BETWEEN THE *people* WHO MAKE IT AND THE *ones* WHO DON'T IS JUST THE *courage* TO BEGIN WHERE YOU ARE.

#chasingthebrightside

Eight

YOU'RE TALL ENOUGH

Believe in yourself and there will come a day
when others have no choice but to believe you.
—MUFASA, *THE LION KING*

When I was in middle school, there was a theme park called Carowinds that was all the rage. If you were in the cool group, you'd go there on the weekends in a group date and hold a boy's hand when you were scared on a ride. And if you were really lucky, your date might win a giant, bright-green, stuffed koala for you that does nothing but take up space and creep you out when you walk back in your room and feel like it moved.

My fanny pack and I were not in the cool group, but that didn't stop me from going to Carowinds on the weekend with my mom and my sister. There was a new roller coaster that had just opened up called Top Gun, and it went upside down—something I had only experienced briefly on the monkey bars.

Everyone at school was talking about riding Top Gun and how *wild* it was. That weekend, my mom packed our Capri Suns and SPF 100 and we headed to Carowinds. When we got there, the line for Top Gun was hours long. My mom suggested we go ride the other rides instead, but I was only there for Top Gun.

As we waited in line, we saw kid after kid run out of the exit like they had just come back from Narnia.

Whoo! That was so dope!

The closer we got to the entrance, the more butterflies I got. We got to the station where you stand against the wall and they see if you meet the height requirement. For this ride, you had to be taller than the other ride requirements because it was like the varsity of all the rides. You had to be *ready*.

My mom, my sister, and I all passed the height test. We loaded into the carriage, then they came by and pushed the bars down over our heads and checked that they were locked. And as soon as I heard the click of the bar lock across my chest, I realized I wanted to be anywhere in the entire world but there. It was like hearing the ice crack on the frozen lake you were walking on. I had to get out.

I couldn't even wet my pants with fear because I was frozen. I couldn't even turn to look at my mom because I wanted to remain perfectly symmetrical within the harness straps. One imbalance of a pigtail and I would be toast.

The cart started to click forward, and the whole crowd "whoo'ed" in unison like a bachelorette party embarking on a Trolley Pub. Except for me, because I was too busy running through the past thirteen years of my life like a scene from a movie where someone is sitting in a dark basement and watching someone they lost on an old film reel dimly projected on the wall. Laughing at the good moments but mainly just adding salt to their popcorn via copious tears.

I was there. I could hear the tape rolling and watch all the moments I'd never have again: volleyball games, birthday parties, Dairy Queen trips, fights with my sister over the front seat, and introspective conversations with my stuffed animal manatee.

Please tell my dog I love her.

As we inched closer to the top, the hoots and hollers of the crowd got louder. I saw nothing but sky, then the carriage tilted forward so we were hovering over the park, then we were released down the roller coaster.

Two thoughts went through my mind in this moment:

1. *If I vomit, where will it land?*
2. *Am I tall enough for this roller coaster?*

Question number one was just a one-time thought. Hasn't really crossed my mind since. But question number two I've carried with me for years, just in a different way. Am I tall enough?

I don't mean literally tall enough (I'm five foot eight), but rather, do I meet the requirements to do whatever it is that I'm doing.

When I started my business, I was constantly questioning if I was supposed to be there. I was young, inexperienced, and didn't understand taxes or what PNL stood for. I kept focusing on all of these things I didn't know and felt like it was pointing me to the label of being unfit or unqualified. A lot of times in my business, I felt like I snuck onto the ride and was waiting for someone to kick me off and tell me I didn't meet the height requirement. In my head, they're telling me I'm not supposed to be here. I'm here on accident, and I need to find my way back to the teacup rides.

PLAY DRESS UP

Some days, when I was starting Headbands of Hope, I felt like I was playing dress up. As a kid, I'd dress up like a doctor or a princess or a gymnast and then try my best to fit the role I was playing. When I got older and started my business, it didn't feel much different. I'd want to be an entrepreneur or a speaker, so I'd do what I could to fit the role, still feeling like someone could just pull back the curtain and see that it was all pretend.

But what if playing dress up isn't such a bad thing? In order for us to step into a role, whether that be pretend or real, we have to make a change within ourselves. Sometimes, making that inner change is easier when we feel like we look and act the part. When I got my first speaking gig, I bought my first ever blazer. It was navy blue from H&M for twelve dollars. I'm still not much of a blazer-wearing type, but it helped me walk out onstage for the first time because I felt like I fit the part.

We can even just try something on and see if it fits. We can dabble down the path of being an entrepreneur and test the waters. We can walk in the room as if we've already received the promotion. We can talk to strangers as if we're running for local office.

Playing dress up on the outside and inside isn't silly or inauthentic or conforming, it's giving ourselves that extra nudge to evolve. It's telling our brain that it's okay if we push ourselves a little bit into new territory.

It can be fun to dream about what's next and who you want to be. But when you actually do it and the wheels start turning and you get your first retailer, or you have too many clients and not enough time, or you get your first non-five-star review, that stuff gets real *quickly*.

All of a sudden normal speed bumps start to feel like monster truck ramps and you have no idea how to land.

AM I QUALIFIED?

I remember when we started getting our first retailers. I didn't have a wholesale website yet, so all of my store orders were done in person. Naturally, my first few stores were in my hometown in North Carolina because that's where I could go door-to-door.

But at this point, I was in New York for a summer internship (since I was still in college). A store from my hometown called me and said they needed more headbands. I told the owner my mom would come by within the week with options for her to purchase.

I had to ship headbands from the warehouse to my mom for her to be able to present to the store. The package arrived a few days late, so my mom went in the store a little over a week after the store owner called me. My mom spent hours and created a *beautiful* display with all of the options. She made it look amazing. She called me about four times before to practice her pitch because she didn't want to mess up.

Afterward, she called me. I was about to hop on the subway from Rockefeller Center back to my dorm.

"Hey, how'd it go?" I said.

She was silent for a few seconds.

"Um . . . not good," she responded, sounding defeated.

How could it not have gone well? They called to place an order! I thought to myself.

"What happened?"

"Well, she said you promised the headbands within the week and you were late . . ."

By two freaking days!!!!

". . . but then she said you started selling headbands to other retailers in the same zip code, and that was just wrong to do that. She said you were in over your head."

I remember standing on the street corner at the top of the stairs to walk down to the subway. The summer sun was blazing on me as I held my phone to my ear and my hand started to shake. It was my biggest fear coming true: I wasn't ready for this, and I was in over my head.

"So did she buy anything?" I mustered to ask.

"No. I'm so sorry, Jess. I really tried."

The image in my head of my mom walking out of that store after being rejected by that woman with the display she spent so much time building still to this day makes my blood *boil*. I've had my fair share of business rough patches before, but this one drives me crazy because my innocent and wonderful mom was involved. Of course, my mom thought it was her fault and I had to explain to her that it wasn't at all. Then a friend called me a few days later and told me that store had tossed all of our headbands in the sale bin and removed the sign about our cause.

But back then, in that moment at the top of the subway stairs, I hung up the phone and my heart started pounding and beads of sweat started to form at my forehead. I looked down at my outfit with my work dress and heels trying to be this *business* woman in New York. And I thought to myself: *Who am I to think I can do this? This is all pretend. Clearly, I'm not qualified to run my own business.*

But here is the trap that's so easy to fall into. We can take one bad experience and make up an entirely new story about ourselves that doesn't serve us or accurately represent what we can do. We can take one thing, one person, one situation that didn't work in our favor and make that the theme song for our confidence. We can tell ourselves that one bad hand places us in the non-expert category, so why try? Well, guess what, you're likely not an expert, and that's great news.

YOU'RE NOT AN EXPERT— AND THAT'S AWESOME

The thought of being unqualified can be debilitating. When we think everything is out of our reach, we'll never even try to reach it.

When I calmed down, I called the store owner and apologized and asked if there was anything we could do to earn her business back. Of course she had some snobby response and said no.

It wasn't until later that I realized how insane the store owner's requests were, but at the time I had nothing to compare it to, so I clearly thought *I* was the one in the wrong. To have a one-week turnaround time for a retailer is a big request. We do it when stores ask us to, but it's definitely not the norm; it's more like a favor that a lot of brands charge extra for. And if a store wants to be the only one in a certain zip code carrying a product, they have to ask for zip code protection, and typically that means a contract and a certain minimum order they have to buy in order to keep their territory. We had none of that and had never even discussed it.

But I'm clearly totally over it.

Regardless, I didn't have that knowledge and I was already pushed out of my comfort zone starting this business, so I felt like every mistake was my lack of experience. But if we focus too much on our lack of experience or qualifications, we'll never give ourselves the chance to evolve because we're so worried whether or not we're supposed to be there.

But *everyone* had to start somewhere. It's crazy to think the teachers who are giving us information were once the students learning it. Or that people in the Tour de France once had to learn how to ride a bike. Or that every big business owner probably started with a lemonade stand or upselling candy at school or something like that.

If we all have to evolve into our roles, there has to be a pretty lengthy learning period because we're not born experts. In fact, even when someone might label us as an expert, it's still a loose term to me.

Claiming that you know everything leaves very little opportunity for new discovery. But claiming that you know less leaves many possibilities for what could be.

There are people out there who know a lot about certain things and that's great. Wikipedia the crap out of the things you find interesting. I've spent hours going down a dark hole on Google trying to learn if dark chocolate is *actually* good for you. Always leave an ellipsis at the end of your studies for possibility, not a period.

One of my favorite things to do is laugh at a newsletter I get every day called HARO, which stands for Help a Reporter Out. Basically, reporters and journalists send out what they're looking for in order to write particular stories they're working on. Then people can submit what they know to hopefully get quoted in the article.

Every once in a while, a good business or social entrepreneur one will pop up and I feel like I can help. But a lot of the time, it's looking for "experts" on the most random stuff.

Here are some of my favorites:

- Working on a piece for a national dining site about chicken nuggets that are actually made with fall vegetables. Contact me with any information.
- Looking to interview a Gen Xer (age 38 to 53) who spends too much money on takeout food, restaurant meals, coffee, and other nonalcoholic drinks.
- Looking to interview people who investigate mysterious subjects like UFOs, cryptozoology, or puzzling phenomena like spontaneous combustion.
- What are some specific flirting techniques from previous generations that people now should bring back? Please provide three or more examples with explanations and historical context for each.
- Looking for chicken keepers to share what they wish they knew before they started chicken-keeping.

I'm just waiting for someone to be like, "Yes! Finally my chance to talk about chicken-keeping." I also love how the flirtation techniques needed to be coupled with historical context. Four score and seven flirtations ago. . .

But thinking about being *qualified* is such a dangerous place to be because it's so important to keep moving forward even when we don't know exactly what we're doing. We can't expect to just hop twelve steps ahead without a few mistakes (or crazy retailers). We can't wait until we feel totally qualified or we'll never get there.

And we also never want to reach a place where we feel like we know it all, which is why it's a benefit not to classify yourself as an expert. When we feel like we've reached a place where we should stop being curious or learning from others, that's a far worse place to be than a beginner. Optimists are open-minded and filled with wonder about what's possible without being sure of what's next.

YOU'RE IN THE GAME

Back in the earlier days of my business, I was always feeling like I wasn't tall enough. I let people treat me like a newbie because that's what I thought I deserved. I remember one time I had just started breaking into the speaking industry to spread my message. I got booked to speak at an event in Florida, and I was so excited. I was traveling to a speaking engagement. How cool is that?!

I was around twenty-one years old at the time, and I was definitely the youngest speaker on the roster that day. The other speakers had fancy websites and best-selling books and enough airline miles to fly Mumford and all of his sons on a European tour.

When I got there, I felt out of my league. I wasn't tall enough for this roller coaster. When we were doing sound checks the day before, one of the other speakers complained that she didn't know the cameras were going to be shooting in HD. (If she had, she would have brought her HD makeup!)

The day of the conference, a limousine picked up the speakers from the hotel to drive them to the venue. The only time I had been in a limo was prom night, and I felt like this was going to be *way* better. I slid into the limo and joined the other speakers, eager and excited to start the day. I was wearing one of our diamond headbands (because of course I wear Headbands of Hope when I speak) and one of the other speakers laughed and said, "I guess I missed the memo that we were supposed to wear a tiara."

If this happened today, I would either just laugh it off or tell him that a good headband would help cover up his receding hairline—depending on my mood of course. But back then, I already felt like I shouldn't be there, so this totally deflated me.

I nervously laughed and responded, "It's my business. The headband, it's my business."

"Oh, you make headbands for your business? That's cute."

I wanted to be *anything* but cute. I wanted to be smart, brilliant, talented, fierce, bold, and able to pick up the tab for everyone at dinner without flinching at the bill (that's literally my dream in life). Once I asked a videographer to redo a video they shot about me because it was entirely focused on me being "cute" and had nothing to do with my brain or talents.

When we pulled up to the venue, I was questioning if I should fake an emergency and just call it a day. I felt like my dress-up time was over. But then I felt my phone buzzing in my purse. It was my newly hired publicist.

"Jess, great news! The *Today Show* wants to do a story about you," she said.

"Wait, what?! About me?"

"Yes! They're flying down in two weeks and will probably shoot for two days. The producer is going to call you this afternoon."

I hung up the phone and felt a surge of energy shoot through my body. At this point, there was no dress up. This was me. And the *Today Show* wanted to do a story on me.

I adjusted my *tiara* and marched into the venue, high-fiving the line of people waiting to get in as I walked by. When I walked in, I looked at the board of the six speakers. There wasn't any rank or anyone's picture bigger than the others. There weren't opening acts and headliners. We were all listed on the board equally. We were all in the game.

Here I was thinking I deserved the scraps when we were all eating at the same table. I was letting myself feel like I wasn't enough, when in fact I was equal. The hierarchy was in my head.

After that I gave the speech that finally made me believe that I was a speaker. I gave the speech that propelled me into speaking more than fifty times a year to hundreds of thousands of people all over the world. I gave the speech that allowed me to create Mic Drop Workshop. I gave the speech that put me on the same speaker lineup as Joe Biden. I gave the speech that eventually made my speaking business so big that I had to expand my team to manage it.

Meanwhile, Tiara-Man stood onstage tossing his books to the audience and begging for Amazon reviews. But who says I'm still bitter? I'm not bitter.

DO IT ANYWAY

Our qualifications are not as important as you think when it comes to roller coasters. We are *all* just trying to figure it out and hoping we make it through the upside down. We can all feel out of place. But we belong in our experiences as much as cereal belongs with milk. If anyone prefers dry cereal, then I will promptly be questioning our friendship.

Think about Mason Ramsey, the eleven-year-old kid whose video of him singing "Lovesick Blues" in the middle of a Walmart went viral. He got a record deal and sang at Coachella! Do you think the canned food aisle was the ideal stage to launch his singing career? No, but it was all he had, so he did it anyway. And now he's the yodeling songbird of our generation.

Do not wait until you think you are tall enough for the roller coaster because you will always come up short. Sometimes the main difference between the people who make it and the ones who don't is just the courage to begin where you are . . . and sometimes that's the canned goods aisle.

One of the biggest challenges is getting comfortable with having your abilities and skill sets a few steps behind you. You will never be able to walk into a new experience being totally prepared and knowing *everything* there is to know, so you need to feel tall enough even when you don't have all the answers. You need to accept the fact that you're a work in progress and do it anyway.

I've seen so many people successfully transform into who they want to be, whether it's an entrepreneur, an acrobat, a speaker, or a musician. Very rarely does it have to do with the tangible skill sets they work so hard to master before they step forward. Their success is a direct result of their confidence to figure out what it takes to get where they want to go. Period.

The people who don't get there are the ones who get held up on the questions: Where do I begin? Am I qualified? Will this be too hard? What if I fail?

Now, I'm not saying successful people never asked themselves these questions or have never had doubts, but these doubts don't debilitate them. They let their passion and purpose take up more airtime in their heads than their fears.

The confidence to go for it is not the absence of fear and doubt, it's the knowledge of risks and the decision to go for it anyway. Confidence breeds when you let the excitement of possibility become bigger than the fear of the unknown. That doesn't mean the fear isn't there, but the fear isn't in the driver's seat. The fear is in the back strapped in a car seat begging for a fruit snack while the excitement is pressing the gas.

I always knew that a lot of successful people were confident. That is a clear connection I (and most people) can make. However, where the confidence is derived from was something I got wrong my whole life. That's what was holding me back.

BET ON YOURSELF

Confidence does not always mean certainty. In fact, in my case it rarely meant certainty. To me confidence means an inner passion burning so big that it mobilizes you to go for it, even when you don't know all the answers.

When I was a kid, I played basketball until my sophomore year in high school, when I realized I'd rather do competitive yo-yo than play basketball because I was awful at it. I grew early, so I was always the taller kid in my grade (which is both why I played basketball and why I didn't date boys). But eventually everyone else caught up and I wasn't considered tall anymore.

I remember a game when we were down by one point with only a few seconds left. We had the ball, and our coach called a time-out. In the huddle the coach was trying to come up with a game plan for which player on the team was going to take the last shot. I remember being in that huddle and in my head praying, *Please, God, if you're listening, do not pass me this ball. In fact, just put me on the bench. Pass it to my mom in the stands before you pass it to me. Please, oh please, give the ball to anyone else but me.*

And in the middle of my prayer one of the girls interrupted the coach and said, "Give me the ball."

Everyone, including the coach, stopped and looked at her.

"I got this, just give me the ball."

The coach put his playbook away and said okay, and we put our hands in and went back out there. I know this would be a way better story if I said that she got the ball and hit the game-winning shot at the buzzer, but I honestly don't remember what happened after that because this was freshman year of high school and I think I was so nervous someone would pass me the ball that I blacked out.

But what I do remember is looking at her confidence in that huddle when she said, "Give me the ball." She had no idea what was going to happen when we walked back out on the court or what the defensive plan was from the other team. But she was confident enough that she knew she could figure it out. She was willing to bet on herself.

I would say one of the most important lessons I've learned the past few years was correcting this lie I told myself my whole life: "The people who do great things are the ones who are naturally gifted, experienced, skillful, and prepared for what's to come."

Now here's the truth: the people who do great things are the ones with the confidence that they will figure it out, no matter what.

So when you tell yourself that you're not the one, maybe you are. When you tell yourself it's not your turn, maybe it is. When you tell yourself *tomorrow*, maybe it's *today*.

Because it's not about being ready for everything life has to throw at you; it's about being confident that you can handle it. It's about asking for the ball. Optimism won't work if we don't believe that we can be the ones to do it. You can delegate your taxes and your house cleaning but you can't delegate your optimistic beliefs. The person with the burning vision will work harder than anyone who's being told what to do.

If everyone has to start somewhere, then why not here?

Don't wait for a long list of tangible skill sets and professional abilities to justify getting on the roller coaster. Being confident isn't changing what we know, it's changing our approach. So even when you don't have it figured out, you must still be *so* confident that you . . .

- make moves toward that start-up.
- parallel park even when there's an audience.
- rock that big hat like it's the Kentucky Derby or the royal wedding.
- write the first chapter of your memoir.
- sign up for the single-people kickball league.
- ask the guy out from the Tuesday night Bike and Brew.
- hire a virtual assistant.
- put your name in the hat as a speaker for a conference.
- do the rope climb at your gym.
- change your own tire.
- ask Santa what *he* wants for Christmas.

Whenever someone asked me what my plan was, I used to think I had to have a long list of calculated ways I was going to achieve my goals. Now my answer is short, simple, and real, and I encourage you to take it to be your answer.

Q: What's your plan?
A: Whatever it takes.

Take It or Leave It

Play dress up. Dress up for the next phase of life that you want. What is it that you want to do or be? Try it on, act like you're there, step into that role, and see what happens.

SOMEONE ELSE'S *success* DOES NOT MAKE YOURS ANY LESS. SOMEONE ELSE'S *failure* DOES NOT MAKE YOU ANY BETTER. THE ONLY METRIC THAT *matters* IS OUR OWN INDIVIDUALITY.

#chasingthebrightside

Nine

FINDING THE WHITE SPACE

We do not need magic to change the world,
we carry all the power we need inside ourselves
already: we have the power to imagine better.
—J. K. ROWLING

Recently my husband and I were invited to a "Wine and Design" night by another couple. We learned that Wine and Design is where you go to a class and paint step-by-step what the instructor is telling the class to paint. Then you drink until the fish you're trying to paint starts looking less like a dog and more like a fish.

We agreed to go and showed up ready to Picasso our way through this class. My husband kept reminding me how he'd rather be doing *anything* else as he wrapped his apron around his waist and started mixing his primary colors. This is the same kind of reaction I get when I turn on *The Bachelor*.

"I can't believe you like this show. It's obviously so staged and not real," he says as he pops the popcorn, reclines in the chair beside me, and makes his bracket for who's going to be in the final-four rose ceremony.

When we arrived at Wine and Design, the couple who invited us was already there, armed and ready to paint the moonlight over the ocean the instructor was showcasing at the front of the room. We later learned that this couple was to Wine and Design what Jake and I were to nachos and *College GameDay*. They designated an entire room in their house for the dozens of paintings they completed at Wine and Design nights. When people asked what they do for fun . . . this was their answer.

Our glasses were full, our palettes were mixed, and our brushes were . . .whatever brushes are supposed to be. The instructor showed us the final product of what we would all be working toward, like a personal trainer showing you a Victoria's Secret model. *This is what we're all here to do. Keep your eyes on the prize, and don't you dare let your black paint touch any other color.*

The first step was thrilling because we had a white canvas sitting in front of us. With the first stroke of our brushes, a wave of adrenaline went down our spines. Maybe it was just me, but that first brushstroke was like the first bite of food after a cleanse. (I assume; I wouldn't actually know. I've made it a whopping four hours doing a fasting cleanse.) The instructor went through step-by-step instructions of what to paint next and which colors to use. One of the people in front of us used too dark a blue on her ocean and almost cried. This stuff was *rigid*.

When we were getting toward the end, I peeked at Jake's canvas; his moon looked like a ball of cheese. But him being from Wisconsin, maybe that's what he was going for.

He stared at his canvas and then back at me and said, "I'm just not really sure where I went wrong."

We both busted out laughing at how awful his moon looked, even though we tried to follow instructions. I grabbed the black paint and painted E.T. and Elliott biking across the moon on my canvas.

The couple looked over in panic. "Are we supposed to do that? Are we supposed to paint E.T.?"

"No," I said softly to try to calm them down, "I'm just doing my own thing."

They looked at each other as if I told them I was adopting a family of kangaroos. Before I could do anything else, I looked over at Jake, who had an evil grin on his face as he was painting Jaws coming out of the water.

The instructor started walking around the class, inspecting all the finished masterpieces. The couple stood beside their work, holding their breath and hoping for a gold star. As she made her way over to Jake and me, I had that feeling of sitting in class when the teacher is passing out grades and you know you bombed.

"Magnificent!" She laughed as she looked at our paintings. Then she asked if she could show the class, and we nodded, very confused. She took pictures of our paintings and put them on her Facebook page.

I'm not going to lie, it felt good to be the teacher's pet. Although Miss Color-Inside-the-Lines was about to throw her merlot on my canvas. We offered to contribute our paintings to their home gallery, but they politely declined.

I learned a few things that night:

- Always check to see if the alcohol is included. It wasn't.
- Blue and yellow make green.
- Wait for paint to dry before painting on top of it.
- A good painter doesn't have to follow the rules; he or she can paint according to their own.

DARE TO BE DIFFERENT

Excellence is not about following what's always been done; it's about finding the white space that hasn't been touched yet. It's finding ways to be different from the rest.

When Domino's started their Paving for Pizza campaign, they paved roads in all fifty states so bumps in the road wouldn't destroy pizza on the way to deliveries. No other pizza delivery company focused on paving roads across America.

Paving for Pizza = differentiation

When Amazon launched Amazon Prime for free two-day shipping and returns, it changed the game and set them apart from other online retailers. Before that, online ordering was like sending an owl to deliver a message for you. Now we hit submit and twelve minutes later we're like, "Where's my blender?!"

Amazon Prime's fast/free shipping + returns = differentiation

Your traditional hammock is great for lounging and reading a book but would be tough to sleep in overnight while being exposed to all the elements. So Lawson Hammock created a hammock with a tent over it so you can zip it up and sleep without worrying that a spider will come to your sleepover.

Tented hammock = differentiation

The creators of Topgolf saw a huge opportunity to turn a traditional driving range into a social hangout spot with golf clubs. You can still try to hit a ball as far as you want to, but now you can do that while eight of your friends sit on couches, eat pretzel nuggets, and drink IPAs while laughing at your swing.

Topgolf's social atmosphere = differentiation

Following directions perfectly is literally like finishing a puzzle. You work so hard to put piece by piece together, only for your finished product to look exactly like the front of the box you've been staring at this whole time. Don't get me wrong, I'm not hating on any of you puzzlers out there; it can be a fun distraction and it's nice to have structure. But when it comes to creating optimistic change in the world, the answer will not have directions or come in a box with all the pieces.

And wine is typically not included.

A lot of what society teaches us is that our worth is in our comparison to someone else. We're told that the only way we offer value is if our product has more value than our competitor's. You have to perform better than the other kids in school to be at the top of your class. Then you have to be better than the other applicants to go to a great college. Then you have to beat out those people to get into a better grad school. Then the same thing happens when you get a job; you have to beat out all the other applicants. Then when you want a promotion, the notion is that you have to outperform all of your colleagues.

But this precedent of measuring ourselves based against other people is setting us up not just for conformity but for lack of innovation and creativity. And not to mention, it's not very fun to live a life based on other people's patterns. When it comes to creating change in the world, it's not about being bigger, faster, or stronger than the person beside you; it's about providing something different from what has been done.

Instead of trying to paint the same sunset as the person beside you, find the white space that's untouched. It's the white space that makes people stop and listen, not the lower price or louder commercial (don't you hate it when one commercial is louder than the other?). Doing things differently gives you your own lane to drive instead of sitting in traffic on the road that everyone else takes. Your lane might not have a map, but at least you're breaking free from the hamster wheel of doing the same thing as everyone else.

CREATE A LEGACY

When I first started Headbands of Hope, I'll be honest with you: I didn't have the best headbands, or the best website, or the best *anything* for that matter. Thinking of the fonts and colors I used on the original site makes me want to cry. I think at one point I made the background of my website a green chevron with blades of grass growing at the top. I was nineteen, running this show out of my dorm room, so give me a break. But the business was still growing every day because I was doing something different from any other headband company out there: I was donating headbands to kids with cancer with every headband I sold.

Headbands donated to kids with cancer = my white space

I was filling white space that no one had noticed yet, and that was what made people come shop. And because we were different, it encouraged people to talk about us and share with friends and family. We weren't just a headband company, we were "the headband company that donates headbands to kids with cancer."

YOU + THE WHITE SPACE YOU FOUND AND FILLED = YOUR LEGACY

What you have to offer that's different is how people will remember you. Maybe it's something as small as a business card with a unique quote on it or as big as a start-up that's filling a need that no one has touched. Or maybe you take a stab at a new way of doing your job that no one has done before. When we're creative and daring enough to be different, we're creating our legacy.

Right now, I'm not talking funeral legacy (although that can be true too); I'm talking about legacy in how someone is remembered and perceived, even if it was five minutes ago. For example, I was at a layover in the Detroit airport and I saw stationary bikes set up in the terminal. Instead of sitting at a restaurant and eating average food and watching a game that you care nothing about to kill time before your flight, you could get a little exercise and people watch while you pedal. It was something I hadn't seen at other airports, so whenever I thought of the Detroit airport, I thought of the stationary bikes.

Another example of how the white space can make you stand out is an interviewer who is conducting interview after interview and remembers the one applicant who left a plant at the front desk with a card that says, "I hope we can grow together."

And that's the girl who got the job (true story). She didn't have better grades than the rest of the candidates or maybe even wasn't as qualified, but she did something different and that's what she was remembered for *and* that's what made them take a risk on her.

Instead of running ourselves into the ground trying to beat the competition, we can become more noticeable and effective by being different.

Being different isn't just about standing out from the crowd, it's also about the sense of innovation and originality people assign to the ones who dare to be different. And it's about assigning that identity to yourself. In every move you take, you can ask yourself: *Is this the best way or just the way it has always been done?*

10-DEGREE TURN

Finding the white space doesn't mean we have to be *drastically* different in our approach to life. A company like Uber did something drastically different by disrupting how we get from one place to the next. Spotify did something drastically different with how we consume music. Whoever invented carrot cake did something drastically different by adding a vegetable to a dessert—who would have thought it would be so delicious?

But you don't have to pull a Lady Gaga and show up to a red-carpet event in a slab-of-meat costume in order to be different. Being different doesn't have to mean doing a 180-degree turn from everyone else, or even a 90-degree turn. Sometimes even just changing something 10 degrees is enough to break patterns and stand out.

Take sandwich shops for example. You have your main players: Subway, Quiznos, Jersey Mike's. They all make pretty much the same sandwiches, but just a little bit differently. Quiznos toasts their subs. Jersey Mike's, my personal fave, shaves the meat right in front of you and dresses the sandwich "Mike's Way"—onions, lettuce, tomato, red wine vinegar, olive oil, and spices. And Subway . . . actually I don't know what separates Subway. They just make sandwiches.

That little bit of difference is usually enough of a difference for someone to wait for the next exit so they can go to their *favorite* sandwich shop. Even the difference between McDonald's and Wendy's is noticeable, despite similar menus. The main difference is Wendy's square burgers and fiery Twitter feed.

Warby Parker allows customers to ship multiple pairs of eyeglasses to try on, then keep the pair they like. They identified a small change to how we shop that makes a big difference in how they're remembered.

TURN HEADS

After Headbands of Hope started rolling, I was looking for new ways to find white space beyond our "headbands to kids with cancer" mission. We were receiving thousands of thank-you letters from hospitals that received our headbands, and I wanted our customers who made this possible to feel the way we felt when we opened these letters.

That's when we started our Donation Confirmation email. Instead of your standard *Your Order Is Complete* email that you get when you order online, we send a follow-up email two weeks after someone places an order with the exact hospital name their donated headbands went to.

We even started doing this same system with our retailers. Their purchases that they make for their store benefit their local children's hospital. It's a small offer of transparency that sets us apart.

At the same time, I was wanting to go to wholesale trade shows to try to get Headbands of Hope carried in more stores. I called around to some other brands I knew to ask if the stores placed orders at the show or if they had given them information to order later. They said that some will place orders at the show, but larger retailers have to run it up the flagpole before they purchase, so they just take information.

When I asked what kind of information they give out at their booths, all of them had stacks and stacks of printed catalogs that they'd hand out to stores. To me, it seemed wasteful with too much paper used, and a pain in the butt to carry and transport.

There was so much information I wanted to give to potential buyers: our product catalog, our press articles, our videos of hospital visits. I couldn't print it all in a catalog, so I went onto Vistaprint and purchased a big box of custom flash drives with the Headbands of Hope logo on them.

Before the show I popped some popcorn, turned on *Planet Earth*, and loaded all of the flash drives with all the information we needed to hand out to the stores, while watching penguins waddle into the abyss.

When I got to the trade show, I put my flash drives into a basket and was ready to reel in some stores. As a new brand, it's sometimes a steeper hill to climb at your first few trade shows because people haven't seen you before. And (I didn't know this at the time) a lot of first-time brands don't survive until the next trade show, so some stores don't even bother until they've seen you attend three or four times.

I could tell some stores were hesitant because they never heard of me before, and I was only twenty-two trying to run a business. But the moment I'd say, "All of our information is on this flash drive for you to review when you get home," it was like someone who doesn't eat bread was about to pass up a pizza and then they heard it was gluten-free. It totally changed the game.

The flash drive was the white space I needed to make people stop and listen. It was what set me apart from the hundreds of catalogs being tossed at them. The flash drive was my sprinkles in a lineup of vanilla cones.

Eventually I saw a buyer walking by, and she had an Ulta name tag. The buyers with the big-store name tags are always getting bombarded by brands at shows because everyone wants to be picked up by a national retailer. Luckily I have no shame and chased her down anyway.

I could tell immediately that she was tuning me out because behind me were a dozen other brands trying to talk to her about their products. But the moment I whipped out the handy-dandy flash drive, she paused and started paying attention to what I was saying.

Three years after that we were carried in all one thousand Ulta locations across the country.

Yes, I know, it took three years. We were almost at the pace of the next Olympics. But still, we did it. Even if it took a while, that flash drive was what put us in the game.

I found a small area of white space in the trade show industry by transforming one thing I thought could be done better, and that was enough to set us apart. The white space is what makes people stop, listen, and remember.

But it's a lot of pressure to come up with "the next big idea." Or it can be daunting to rack your brain for things that haven't been done before. Let me try to ease your mind.

In 1889, Charles H. Duell, the commissioner of the US Patent Office, thought the Patent Office would shrink and eventually close because, "Everything that can be invented has been invented." Little did he know that the world was still waiting on iPhones, press-on nails, fanny packs, fidget spinners, and the Squatty Potty. Nice try, Charles.

Everything we know now as "normal" was once a novel idea. But it took someone mixing chocolate in their milk to figure out a new way of life (yes, I consider chocolate milk a way of life). One morning someone was sick of needing eggs or vegetable oil to make their pancakes, so they created the complete pancake mix that only requires water to cook heavenly flapjacks. Our ideas don't have to be revolutionary to matter. Sometimes they just need to improve on something that already exists.

And think, if that was not true the world would never have been gifted the Shake Weight.

Let's take the complexity out of being different. Rid yourself of the pressure to create the next Spotify, Airbnb, or singing contest reality TV show (how many of those can we have?). Instead, just think about the last time you were frustrated about something. Frustrated that your favorite food has too many calories, or frustrated that you forgot to turn on your Crock-Pot and you were already at work, or frustrated that no one is selling the exact kind of shoes you want.

Well maybe there's a way you can make a less-calorie version of your favorite food. Or maybe you should be able to control your Crock-Pot from your phone. Maybe you could design and create the shoes that you want.

INSPIRATION FROM FRUSTRATION

Frustration signals to us that something could be better. It tells us when there are inefficiencies or gaps in the market. Instead of just getting mad, what if we followed that frustration to fill that white space? What if all the moments when we wished there was something inspired us to create it?

Finding the white space can be simplified by taking a proactive approach to the things we wish were different. I wished that there was a company that gave headbands to kids with cancer, but there wasn't; so I created one. And someone out there wished there was a Christmas sweater for dogs, but there wasn't; so he or she created it. And for that, I am grateful.

But there's also not enough time in the day to create *everything* we wish existed, so we have to pick and choose to create the things that are worth the tenacity and effort it takes to ruffle the feathers of tradition.

Here are some ideas I wish existed but haven't had the time to create:

- A dog translator device
- A deodorant or spray that stops my armpit from sweating. (Yes,

I said *armpit*, singular. I only sweat out of my right armpit. I've been told I'm a medical marvel.)

- A bra that you can store your phone, money, ChapStick, and keys in
- A way to sneak your seventy-pound dog on a plane
- A hammock that's easy to get in and out of
- A button that makes the guy next to you on the plane stop hacking out his lungs
- A night mouth guard that still makes you semi-desirable
- A "hangry" detector that immediately sends you the coordinates of the nearest Chipotle
- A stationary bike that unlocks your Netflix shows by pedaling
- An SOS app that triggers a phone call from your mom to get out of an awkward conversation

If any of these exist already, let me know. And if they don't, knock yourself out creating it, and hit me up when you do.

HATERS GONNA HATE

When we create something new or go against the norm, we run the risk of traveling a road with no road map. It's just us and our intuition, which can be a scary and beautiful place to be. There's no cookbook for the recipe you want to create, so you might have to grab everything in your pantry, toss it in a pot, and hope it comes out edible. And you also might have to do that twelve more times to get closer to where you want to go. But when we break the patterns of tradition, that's when true change happens.

But one thing that took me a long time to understand was that not *everyone* is on board with different. Don't expect for there to be a sandwich named in your honor right off the bat because some people are uncomfortable with different.

Not everyone will be cheering you on as you paint Jaws coming out of the water in your Wine and Design class. Some people do not appreciate when you dive into the white space, and all will not celebrate you as you march down a wild path that you're paving as you go. Some people will tell you you're crazy and to come back and take the highway like everyone else. Others will try to tell you that you can't make it.

I was totally blindsided by this when I first started Headbands of Hope. I naively thought that every time I told someone what I was doing, they'd throw a parade in my honor or make T-shirts with my face on them. But some people were hurtful, and I didn't understand why.

One business professor I met with for advice told me, with his feet kicked up on his desk, "At most, this will turn into a fad for a year and then fizzle out. You might be better off not wasting your time."

He. Said. That.

But being nineteen years old and having a professor tell you something like that reminds me of when I realized the tooth fairy wasn't real. You start to question all of your efforts and ability and wonder if they're right. Maybe going uphill isn't worth it?

What took me a long time to figure out (and I'm still figuring it out) is why people try to bring you down. People in their own comfort zones tend to resent the people who break outside theirs. It's really easy for someone to stand safely on the shore and point out how stupid your unicorn raft is out at sea. But at the end of the day, they're the ones who never left shore, and that is not your problem.

Anna Wintour, legend in the fashion industry and editor in chief at *Vogue*, was fired from *Harper's Bazaar* because she was told her shoots were too edgy.

Modeling agencies told Marilyn Monroe she should consider being a secretary instead of a model.

They were different and some of the world wasn't ready for it, but their success goes to show that their differences were what made them great. Most of the time, someone's negativity toward you is more about their frustration with their own story than it is about yours. We can't control this (as much as I've tried). And better yet, our time is better spent actually making the change happen than convincing people that it's right. And people who only live in *their* patterns will always stand in your way.

When you want to do something big, expect someone to tell you that you're small. Then do it anyway.

COMPARISON TRAP

One thing I feel is important to note here is that sometimes *we* are the haters of our own ideas and ambitions. Sometimes we are the ones saying that a Christmas sweater for dogs is a stupid idea. Have you ever talked yourself out of trying something new, being adventurous, or starting something because fear and comparison set in? These stories we tell ourselves are often more debilitating toward our ambition and goals than other people are. The stories we tell ourselves matter. And that is also why comparing our ideas with others' will rarely be healthy.

In fact, most judgments about ourselves are in relation to someone else. Isn't that crazy? Anytime I'm hard on myself, I can usually connect it to feeling less than someone else, not because of my own personal standards. It's a flaw I'm working on.

So as I'm telling this to you, I'm also telling this to me.

The more we compare ourselves to everyone else, the more we feel we have to be like them. The more we feel we have to be like them, the less daring we will be to be different and find the white space. It's impossible to be proud of your individuality if your metric of success is based on someone else.

We can't compare our chapter 1 to someone else's chapter 7. What we see across from us on the subway, on Instagram, or parked in people's driveways are not a good metric for how we're doing . . . because we only see what people are willing to expose. We don't see all the things we're not willing to admit: the crumpled papers, the failed attempts, the Spanx, the dental crowns, the jeans sewn at the crotch.

Someone else's success does not make yours any less. Someone else's failure does not make you any better. The only metric that matters is our own individuality.

BE ON YOUR OWN TEAM

When it comes to doing something different, we have to be on our own team. We have to cheer ourselves on and not wait to get a thumbs-up from the rest of the population. In fact, we have to be okay if they give us a different finger. The guys who started Airbnb had a tough time getting funding to start their business because no one believed in their idea. Why? Because there was nothing to compare it to. It hadn't been done yet. But clearly their story proves that just because it hasn't been done doesn't make it a bad idea. In fact, it could be a $30 billion idea.

Some people told me Headbands of Hope wouldn't work. Some people told me I was too young. Some people told me I'd be better off getting a *real* job first. Some people told me I needed a cofounder who knew what he or she was doing. Some people told me I needed investors and I'd never be able to fund growth myself.

But guess what? Some people don't know what they're talking about.

Some people will try to make your beautiful differences feel like flaws. But they're not. We have to be on our own team and cheer louder for ourselves instead of waiting for a crowd to form.

Optimism sometimes means manifesting things that aren't there and creating what hasn't been created yet. In a world that's constantly changing and evolving, we have to keep up with what's good for it. Sometimes what's better isn't what was better twenty years ago or isn't what everyone else is doing. We have to stay on our toes and be willing to create our own playground if the one we want doesn't exist.

Whether it's as big as starting a company to fulfill a need or as small as drawing E.T. on your canvas at Wine and Design, finding and filling the white space is something everyone should try. Even if it doesn't work out (which has happened to me many times), you're still rewiring your brain to think differently than what's already been done. There's no room for comparison when you're in the white space. You're pushing the walls of your comfort zone to find even the slightest comfort in being different.

And in a world of multiple choice and standardization, your differences are exactly what we need.

Take It or Leave It

Think about the routines and patterns you do every day. What's a pattern you could break to practice being different? Maybe instead of sending your regular typed email response, you send a video message back. Or maybe instead of sitting in traffic going to work every morning, you leave a little earlier and read a book on the bus.

GOOD DOESN'T HAVE TO BE *recognized* IN ORDER FOR IT TO *work* OR BE WORTH IT. IT CAN JUST BE GOOD.

#chasingthebrightside

Ten

THE WORST FUND-RAISER EVER

Be someone who makes someone
else look forward to tomorrow.
—UNKNOWN

Before I got an office for Headbands of Hope, I'd work out of the local coffee shop every day. I'd pack my bag in the morning with my computer and a Ziploc full of Pirate's Booty and head to the "office" of java and scones. (P.S., if you don't know what Pirate's Booty is, it's heaven's cheese puffs. If you have never had them, please feel free to take a break from reading, go buy a bag, and pick this back up where you left off . . . I'll wait.) I loved the energy of being out in the open, working on my business, and watching people hustle in and out throughout the day, picking up the wrong mobile orders, all working on their own thing. Since I was a one-woman show in the beginning, working from coffee shops made me feel as if I was a part of something, like I had a place in the work world. It also forced me to wash my hair and look halfway decent, so there's that too.

One day I was sitting in the coffee shop, typing away on my latest Headbands of Hope blog post for my readership of seven people, when a woman came up to me. She noticed the Headbands of Hope bumper sticker on the front of my computer.

"I saw you guys on the news last night! I love what you're doing for the kids."

We had been featured in a small segment on the local news the day before and this was my first "public sighting," so I was *thrilled*. I wondered when I'd get the call for my reality television show: *The Headband Harem.*

"Thank you! We were so excited to get our story out there . . ." to the viewership of Raleigh who happened to be watching the news from 3:07 to 3:10 p.m. the day before.

She told me to keep up the good work and I thanked her and kept typing away on my computer, but now with more pizzazz because I had just been recognized in public.

A few minutes later, she came by again and said, "You do so much for others, it's time someone does something for you." Then she dropped a white envelope on my computer and left before I could say anything.

Could it be tickets to a concert? A letter of encouragement? A picture of a puppy? A coffee gift card? I opened up the envelope and it was like opening an undiscovered chest from the *Titanic*. Inside was $1,000 cash.

No note, no anything. Just cold. Hard. Cash.

My heart started racing. I couldn't believe it. I looked for her outside in the parking lot, but she was gone. Just like in the movies. I could never find her to thank her. I know this is a long shot, but if you're the woman who gave me that envelope six years ago and you're reading this: *thank you!*

As someone who was still measuring the Scotch packing tape to prevent going over budget, $1,000 was a huge push for my business at the time. However, she did something bigger than dropping $1,000 on my laptop. She inspired me to think more about what I can do for others.

If optimism is about envisioning something good, then practicing small gestures of *doing* good is like training camp for optimism. If we get in the habit of reacting with an open heart, then we're developing a habit of optimism.

SMALL GESTURES WITH A BIG IMPACT

But there was one problem: I was not at a point in my life where I could drop an envelope with $1,000 on someone's desk. Shoot—I couldn't even be the tooth fairy at that point. I was still taking home my free to-go coffee refill at the end of the day so I could heat it up the next morning. I was still riding off of anyone's Netflix account I could get access to (including ex-boyfriends'). I was still planning my weekends based on Groupon deals. I was *not* in a place to drop $1K as a little warm and fuzzy on a Tuesday morning for anyone—unless it was to my landlord for rent.

But believe it or not, my own company helped me find the right mind-set for giving back. Here I was giving out these small, simple accessories of headbands. I wasn't going from room to room paying off hospital bills or renovating houses *Extreme Makeover: Home Edition* style. I was giving a *small* gesture that was making a *big* impact.

A headband was something small but powerful. The gesture behind it was bigger than the product itself. I wanted the headband to translate a message of hope, beauty, color, confidence, or anything that a patient needed a little more of at the time.

One of my favorite stories was from a nurse at one of the children's hospitals we donate to. She told me that whenever a patient chooses to shave her head (because the hair is falling out too much due to chemotherapy), she always puts one of our headbands on the patient before she turns her to the mirror. She says the headband softens the harshness of the immediate shock of seeing themselves without any hair.

It gives them a reason to smile.

Another time I went into a hospital and sat down at a patient's bed as she picked out a headband. I saw her Mickey Mouse blanket and told her about my time working at Disney World and asked what her favorite characters were. She told me Mickey, Goofy, and Donald Duck. So naturally, I started quacking like Donald Duck, and she started laughing (definitely *at* me, not *with* me, but I was cool with it). I looked out her door and saw a small crowd had formed with her parents and the hospital staff, and some of them were crying.

When I walked out I said, "Is everything okay? Why are you guys crying?"

Her mom said, "We've been in the hospital for more than a month now and this is the first time she's talked to anyone."

And that's what a simple gesture can do. I can't give $1,000, but I can give a reason to smile and talk.

We hear a lot about the Ellen DeGeneres–style giving that involves a massive check to charity or sending a kid to college who couldn't afford it. Or funding a new jungle for endangered species to live in. All of that is awesome, and kudos to you if you can do that. But giving back doesn't require a big fat check; it requires a big fat heart.

When we focus on a mountain of trash, we don't see the single piece sitting right in front of us that we could easily pick up and throw away. We're too fixated on the impossible task of picking up *all* the trash, instead of the small but very possible tasks that are right in front of us.

Optimism doesn't mean you have to revolutionize the world. Optimism is about a perception of the world that influences positive behaviors, big or small.

You know when you're at the grocery store and you're just trying to buy some celery (okay, they're chocolate-covered pretzels) and the person in front of you has a cartful like they're preparing for a hurricane, so they let you go in first? *That* is giving back.

You know when you're at a restaurant and your waitress has been awesome and you bump your tip up a few extra dollars than the standard? *That* is giving back.

You know when your friend lost her job and you bring over dinner and watch *Keeping Up with the Kardashians* to help her perk up? *That* is giving back.

Having a heart to make the world better starts with the person right in front of you. How can you make his or her life better? How can you help just *one* person today? Right now, in this moment, you don't need to focus on how to stop a meteor from hitting planet Earth. If that's your job, then I totally want to be friends with you and learn more. But if it's not, don't stress about it. Just focus on finding those moments in the day where we can put ourselves second, even just briefly.

If you can't give a rotisserie chicken, then give a chicken nugget. Thank you for coming to my TED Talk.

KARMADILLO

When I was a kid and someone was mean, my mom would always talk about karma—what goes around comes around. She has a *rooted* belief in karma. If that kid swiped your Snack Pack, then he's destined for a life of misery. If that girl told you you're too fat to be a cheerleader, then no one will come to her birthday party ever again. It was like an equation of the universe: be good, good will come your way. Be bad, then strap on a helmet because it's about to go down.

To me good karma means I'm influencing the future collision points in my life to be positive ones, because I'm placing myself in positive situations and around positive people.

One time I saw a story on the internet about a guy who tried to shoot an armadillo and the bullet bounced back and shot him in the leg. Someone commented, "Karmadillo," and I haven't been able to forget it since. Now whenever I see someone being difficult or selfish, I whisper under my breath *karmadillo*, and I'm just waiting for someone to hear me and ask me to explain. I'm ready.

We don't have to go deep into beliefs in karma and hakuna matata stuff to realize that our chances of good things happening to us go up when we build our world on the principle of doing good things.

It's like optimism on autopilot. Take for example the Starbucks pay-it-forward story in Pittsburgh. One person in the drive-through paid for the person behind them. Then, more than 130 cars later, people were still paying for the order behind them. One generous act can be a ripple effect for further good. When someone does something nice for you, do you ever walk away feeling inspired to do something nice for someone else?

The medium we choose doesn't have to be money (or coffee); it can be making them smile, making a part of their day a little bit easier, creating opportunity for them or a joke you know they'll think is funny. It means recognizing little collision points in our lives as opportunities to create good.

I do believe we all have an innate part of us that wants to do good and help others. But society gives so much airtime to money as the only currency for worthy causes. Nonmonetary ways of giving don't receive the same amount of attention or even have the proper ecosystems to encourage more giving. With monetary giving, there are fancy charity galas with big-ticket costs and boards ticking up with donations throughout the evening. I've been to these and they do amazing work for charities, but it also just focused on one medium of giving: money.

People who aren't the coffee shop hero and can't drop $1,000 checks onto laps of strangers feel like they can't attend these kinds of money-driven events. And when you're told that the way to give is through monetary donations, it feels like you can't contribute at all if donating money isn't an option for you.

DOESN'T HAVE TO BE DOLLARS

My friend Joey and I were discussing this concept of charity galas one day. He has a charity called The Monday Life, where you sign up to donate a dollar every Monday to enhance the lives of childhood cancer patients. Just a dollar. The idea behind his organization is that Mondays won't be so bad if you know you're giving back, even just a dollar.

We bonded over the fact that both of our ideas were powered by small acts of kindness generating big influence. Then we took it a step further: What if we could give this style of giving the same kind of celebration as a traditional charity gala?

So we decided to do just that: an evening where people offer acts of kindness instead of money for patients and families at the local children's hospitals. To take it a step further, we banned money entirely. We called the event Give Gala: The Worst Fund-Raiser Ever . . . because we raised zero dollars.

The first year we did it, we had more than five hundred people get dressed up and come out to Give Gala. Thanks to great community sponsors, we were able to offer the same kind of atmosphere as the other charity galas: hors d'oeuvres, open bar, music, dancing, and even acrobats.

In order to register, you had to offer an act of kindness for patients and families at the local children's hospital. Here were some of my favorite offers:

- hand-lettering lessons,
- cooking meals for a family,
- dog walking,
- car washing,
- babysitting so the parents can have a night out,
- knitting lessons,
- a princess unicorn birthday party on their farm,
- tickets to a football game,
- family photos,
- a yoga class,
- a haircut + makeup session.

But I would say this was my favorite:

- a free, private performance of a blend of cool jazz, traditional Appalachian music, and Gypsy and Latin styles with an all-acoustic lineup from the Cool String Concept.

Hey, you never know what people are into.

We compiled a list of everything offered and sent it to the patients and families at the local hospitals, then connected the people who wanted to take them up on an offer. That was where the real magic happened.

At one Give Gala, a little boy from the hospital who loved fire trucks attended. A firefighter came to the venue to pick him up in a vintage fire truck and take him on a ride. Another year there was a boy from the hospital who wanted to wear a tux to the Give Gala. He had never worn one before, and his mom said he wanted to go full James Bond. They went to Men's Wearhouse to rent a tux and when his mom told the sales associate what the tux was for, he gave the boy and his dad matching tuxedos for free!

At Give Gala last year, a family offered their beach house, which they use as a rental property, for a family who needed a getaway. I later learned that the family who accepted the offer is now great friends with the family who offered their place. They even spent New Year's Eve together!

This year, we had a teen patient who wanted to be a YouTube influencer, so we matched her up with someone at the event who is an influencer with a massive following. We also had a kid who wanted to start a food truck with his family's mac and cheese recipe, and someone at the event had a food truck business and helped him get started.

Each year, Give Gala gets bigger and bigger. But my hope for Give Gala isn't just to have one evening where people think about what they can offer. I want the concept of Give Gala to be a reminder that no act of kindness is too small, and we should never take ourselves out of the giving equation, no matter our financial status or how busy we are.

The no-money concept of Give Gala forces people to look beyond what's in their wallets and think about what else they can offer someone. Whether that be skills, resources, talents, or even just your time.

Giving back can have the connotation of being all hearts and flowers; that if we just give instead of receive, then all will be good in the world! All of our problems will float away, like the balloons we just dropped off at the nursing home. But that's not always the case.

IT'S NOT ALWAYS HEARTS, FLOWERS, AND FRAPPUCCINOS

Believe it or not, giving back is still something I have to actively think about.

A lot of people think because of the philanthropic nature of my company that I must be the Mr. Rogers of our generation, but it's not that easy (and puppets freak me out). Every opportunity to do something good is an active choice. And sometimes, although I hate to admit it, I make the wrong choice. Sometimes I think getting home five minutes earlier is way more important than letting someone go in front of me in line.

Here's what people don't say that I'm going to say anyway: giving is *hard*. It's hard to think beyond your needs and put yourself in someone else's shoes. It's hard to put yourself second. It's hard to get to a headspace where you can justify sacrificing this innate survival mode that puts you first. And it's hard to use your time and resources for something that you may never see.

Because that's the other thing about giving: the results of kindness have nothing to do with recognition and everything to do with intention.

It was mind-blowing to me that the woman at the coffee shop could just drop $1,000 like that and not want an awards ceremony or a Frappuccino named after her. It got me thinking: if you hold the door for someone and they don't say thank you, does it mean you shouldn't have held the door? Or if someone's meter is about to run out and you see they're going to get a ticket, should you drop coins in even if they'll never know it was you?

Once there was a homeless man outside of the grocery store that my husband and I were walking into. He asked for cash, but we told him we'd get him some groceries. We went in and got bread, peanut butter, jelly, chips, and some other food for him and put it in a bag and gave it to him outside. He looked in the bag, looked at us, and said, "I wanted wheat bread."

You know those viral videos where someone does something nice for someone and the recipient starts crying and tells that person they're the sole reason for their faith in humanity and good on this earth? Well, that doesn't happen all the time. Refer to exhibit A: Wheat Bread Man.

But does that mean the next person we see outside the grocery store shouldn't get the chance to be the recipient of something good? If we base our intentions on the acknowledgement, thank-yous, or approval of others, then we won't have any spirit to give.

I likely will never have the chance to say thank you to the woman who dropped $1,000 onto my laptop that day, but the recognition of the act didn't influence the magnitude of the result. She changed my life, regardless of whether or not I can tell her that.

SILENTLY FULFILLED

Good doesn't have to be recognized in order for it to work or be worth it. It can just be good. We can't expect a standing ovation every time we extend ourselves for someone else. We also can't let that be the reason to lend a helping hand. We have to be *silently* fulfilled.

If we see a plastic bag in the park that the birds are trying to eat, we need to pick up the bag and walk it to the trash. There won't be a red carpet and the birds will most likely not say thank you. But if the *intent* is to serve, then we need to be okay with the silence.

Recognition doesn't change the result. Sometimes I catch myself veering off from this. With the nature of what we do at Headbands of Hope, it's important to show our audience the impact of their purchase with pictures and video from our hospital donations. But sometimes we're not allowed to take pictures. I catch myself having a moment where I'm frustrated, but then I realize the pictures and recognition don't change the result. I'm still showing up and giving headbands and spending time, no matter if there are cameras there or not.

OPTIMISM INTO ACTION

If optimism is our vision of good, then what power does optimism have without action? Right now, in this moment, I'm not talking about building your do-good empire. I'm talking about finding the small points of your day where you can train yourself to lead with compassion and action to make the world better. Because compassion is to optimism like a hammer is to a nail. Without a hammer, the nail doesn't work. And without compassion, optimism can't exist. We have to genuinely care in order to want to help.

If you're stumped on where to give, think about the things you like doing, or the things that people thank you for. Do you like cooking? Gardening? Making crafts? Playing basketball? Whatever it is that you like doing, think about how you can use those things to serve. Can you cook for a soup kitchen? Help out in the city garden? Make crafts at a nursing home? Can you be a volunteer coach for a youth basketball league?

Or drop $1,000 on someone's laptop? That works too.

Take It or Leave It ....

In the next twenty-four hours, do a silent gesture of giving. Something that no one will know you did. Whether that's throwing coins in someone's parking meter, paying for another order at the drive-through, dropping flowers on someone's doorstep, anonymously contributing to someone's GoFundMe or Kickstarter campaign, or going to your closest teacher supply store and leaving money for the next teacher who walks in to get school supplies for his or her class.

IF THE VOICES IN OUR HEADS *control* THE WAY WE WALK THROUGH LIFE, THEN WE NEED TO *Train* THEM TO SAY *yes* TO THE LIFE WE WANT AND *no* TO THE LIFE WE DON'T.

#chasingthebrightside

Eleven

THE THINGS WE TELL OURSELVES

Thinking "here goes nothing" could
be the start of everything.
—DREW WAGNER

I was backstage getting ready to speak to three thousand college students from all across the country. At this point, I had been speaking pretty regularly, and nothing really threw me. I've had someone bring a dog that started barking, someone light up a cigarette in the middle of my talk, and I've even had Vice President Joe Biden run over on his talk so mine started late. But that was still a win for me because I got to say, "The vice president ran into my talking time."

But for some reason at this particular talk, one of the backstage staff members asked a question that threw me.

"Hey, what song do you want to walk out to?" he asked.

"What do you mean?"

"The song. We play a song as you walk out onto the stage. What song do you want it to be?"

I paused for minute. It wasn't abnormal for them to play music as I walked out onstage; I had just never been asked what song I wanted them to play before.

"Bruno Mars. 'Treasure.' Except skip the weird part in the beginning about a squirrel and go straight to the chorus."

"Got it," he said and put his headset back on.

My husband took me to a Bruno Mars concert one year for my birthday when we were dating. We were broke college kids so the tickets were in the nosebleed section, but I may as well have been one of his backup dancers onstage with the way I was dancing. My husband had to move down a couple of seats so I could have more range of motion. Something about that song made me feel like I had wings; everyone needed to watch out because I was about to fly.

Back at the speaking engagement, I was waiting for my cue to enter. "Now!" the guy said in a loud whisper as he motioned me to move onto the stage.

As I took my first step into the bright lights, the song started playing, and I felt more confident than a bachelorette party singing "Lady Marmalade" at karaoke. I was unstoppable.

The music faded and I gave one of my best talks I've ever delivered. Afterward I couldn't help but replay that question in my head, *What song do you want to walk out to?*

You might not have that option in such a literal sense, but every day when we wake up we pick the song we want to walk out to. Think about when your alarm goes off: you put your feet on the ground, you walk to the bathroom, and you're brushing your teeth. For me, that's my moment when I'm looking in the mirror, running through my day in my head until my Sonicare tells me I've brushed enough. And in that moment, that's when I decide what my song is going to be, because we always have a choice of how we're going to approach our day.

We pick the lyrics, the chorus, and the tempo. We pick whether or not we're walking out to Bruno Mars, Metallica, a techno track with dope bass drops, or a slow, sad country song about how the fish aren't biting today.

Have you ever been in a spin class or on a run and you're losing steam and you approach a hill and you think to yourself, *Maybe I'll just call it a day and place my mobile order for my grande vanilla latte at Starbucks?*

And then the song changes, and with that first beat you change too. You look at that hill and now you're ready to go harder than a Serena Williams forehand on a match point. Before you know it, that hill is just a warm-up for what you're about to do next.

Imagine if we exercised that same amount of control with the music we play in our heads and in our lives. With every challenge we face, with every new beginning, with every win or loss, and with every time we open our eyes to a new day, we pick the song.

And the way we can do that is by getting familiar with the voices in our heads.

THE VOICES IN OUR HEADS

You have this voice in your head that dictates your every move. And when I say "the voice in your head," I don't mean the weird and creepy "I hear voices that aren't there" kind of voice. We have enough voices in our heads telling us we can't accomplish our dreams. In fact, we have on average seventy thousand thoughts a day.[6] And unfortunately, according to behavior psychologists, an average of 77 percent of our thoughts are *negative*.[7]

We have a bad habit of letting the voices in our heads crush our ideas faster than I can crush a three-piece chicken strip combo meal from Chick-fil-A, and if that doesn't mean anything to you, just know it means *fast*.

The voices in our heads are *everything*. Our emotions, moods, beliefs, and behaviors all stem from them. They are our internal dialogue.

But what I mean by "the voices in our heads" is our internal dialogue with our feelings, decisions, and actions. We're not just out in this world aimlessly reacting to anything and everything without thought. We can have a buffer in our heads that puts a space between our world and how we feel and respond to it. We have a conversation with ourselves just like we'd have with a friend, and that buffer is the voice in our heads that tells us when:

- we can or can't.
- we're too old or too young.
- we're too busy or too bored.
- we're too tall or too short.
- we're ready or not.

FIGURE IT OUT

The first time I realized the power of positive internal dialogue was when I accidentally became a water aerobics instructor one summer in college. I had finished my certification to teach group fitness classes, although I had taught only a cycle class that semester. A country club not far from my house had fitness classes, so I went over with my résumé and asked if they needed any cycle instructors for the summer. The fitness director had two classes she needed a cycle instructor for that she said I could teach, but I was hoping to be teaching at least four or five times a week so I could make more money.

"Do you teach water aerobics?" she asked.

"No," I responded with a slight pause, "but I could figure it out."

She told me I could teach a class that following week and see how it goes. I ran home, opened up Google, and typed *How to teach water aerobics*.

I bought three books on Amazon about water aerobics and had them rush-shipped to my house. That weekend, I read all three books, blasted Justin Timberlake in my living room, and practiced my routines.

Step. Flutter. Splash. Jump!

The following week I arrived to the pool with my boom box, mix CD, water shoes, sunscreen, and visor (yeah, I was killing it) and greeted a pool full of smiling women over the age of sixty-five. I rubbed some sunscreen on my face and plugged in my boom box next to the waterslide and looked out onto the pool.

Could I do this? *But I've never taught water aerobics before. I've never even been to a class*, I thought to myself.

I took a deep breath and changed the voice in my head. *Yes, I can do this. I am a water aerobics instructor.*

"Hey, ladies! I'm Jess and I'm going to be your instructor today. You guys ready to rock?!"

Woooooo!

They all splashed and cheered like they were in the front row at a Beatles concert.

I pressed play and the music started to thump. "Let's start with a march!" I said as I started marching. Then I saw the country club lady who interviewed me sitting under an umbrella sipping lemonade and watching me.

I kept saying to myself: *I'm a water aerobics instructor. I'm a water aerobics instructor.* And then I'd look into the pool and see the women working out, splashing, and having a good time. The voice in my head got louder the more I believed it. *I am a water aerobics instructor.* This wasn't just a role I was pretending to play; this was a profession. I know it sounds ridiculous, and looking back I could tell myself it was *just* water aerobics. But at the time, it was a huge turning point for me to recognize the power of the voice in my head.

Just a week prior, I had only used a pool to practice my handstands or as an excuse to lie on a float that looked like a slice of pizza. But I had set my sights on something that was important to me and figured out how to get from A to B. "A" being "What the heck is water aerobics?" and "B" being "Hi, I'm a water aerobics instructor."

When I finished the class, I felt like Taylor Swift closing out a concert, proudly looking into the pool of happy, sweaty students. I got the job, so I was teaching water aerobics three times a week and cycle two times a week. My water aerobics class got so popular that they had to open up another lane of the pool so all the attendees could fit. On top of that, the women consistently tried to set me up on dates with their grandsons, which I didn't hate. Although none of the dates were successful, I still appreciated the effort of the Pool School (that's what we called ourselves).

Besides the bad dates, I had made an adjustment in my sails that started a slow turn in my mind-set. I realized I could be whatever I wanted to be. Whatever I wanted to do, I could figure it out if I decided it was important to me. I would just tell myself that I could. It wasn't about walking in being a seasoned water aerobics instructor; it was about knowing in my head that I could figure it out. Over the years I realized that most people who did something daring and great first started with their voice. They had to tell themselves that they could.

Optimism is not as much about a tactical plan of execution as it is about internal belief. We can have all the steps laid out on a pretty document that smells like roses. I can buy all the books about water aerobics, but at the end of the day I have to believe that I can do it.

A study on athletes compared instructional self-talk (where athletes remind themselves of specific things to do to play better) and motivational self-talk (self-talk that keeps people on task). They found that positive self-talk was the greatest predictor of success. People didn't need to remind themselves *how* to do something as much as they needed to tell themselves that they are doing something *great*.[8]

If the voices in our heads control the way we walk through life, then we need to train them to say yes to the life we want and no to the life we don't. Just like we teach kids not to repeat the f-bomb we accidentally dropped in front of them, we have to teach ourselves to have a healthy internal dialogue that mobilizes us to go for it, rather than paralyzing us with insecurities.

TRAINING OUR INTERNAL DIALOGUE

But here's the good news: we have more control than we think when it comes to controlling our inner dialogue. It might seem crazy that we can control our thoughts, but we can. We can reprogram our heads as if they were 1995 PCs with a bunch of viruses so that they're sleek new MacBook Pros that don't even know what buffering is.

And guess what? The first step to changing our internal dialogue is *believing* what I just told you.

1. Understand that you have the power to control your thoughts.

The first step to changing your internal dialogue is knowing that your negative thoughts don't have to be your reality.

A lot of our thoughts are formed out of repetition, like an annoying radio commercial that you've heard a million times. But you can change the channel. You can re-record. You can throw away the tapes of the stories we've been telling ourselves for years that don't serve us anymore. You can change the voice in your head.

Maybe you've told yourself for years that you can't go to nursing school because you don't like blood. And even though the career of being a nurse appeals to you, you keep saying in your head, *But I can't do blood.*

But what if you had one bad experience in school where a kid skinned his knee and it made you queasy, and ever since then you've just repeated something to yourself and made it a strong belief, even if it's not? Maybe that was just *one* experience, but you're actually fine with blood and can handle it. And maybe, just maybe, you'd be an awesome nurse wiping up people's blood and slapping a bandage on them like it's your job, because it can be your job if you change the voice in your head.

When things repeat, we mistake them for truth. Sometimes we believe things not because we have a reason but because it's familiar. Recognizing that the voice in your head (even if it is loud and repetitive) is not always true *and* we have the power to change it: that is the first step toward actually changing it.

Better yet, when you really understand the voice in your head, you can learn your triggers. Kind of like my dog when the Amazon delivery guy comes to my house (which is too often) and he hears the beeping from scanning the packages and goes absolutely *nuts*. So then whenever he hears beeping, he assumes it's another one of my boxes of Dawn dish soap because going to the store is *so* 2015.

We each have our own triggers to negative thoughts that we don't even know are there because they're so repetitive that we think they're true. For me, anytime my accountant or advisor wanted to talk numbers for the business, I'd clam up and say to myself, *I'm not good with numbers*. Therefore, I would retreat, not ask questions, and feel stupid when I didn't understand something.

But now when I catch myself doing that, I think, *Is that really true? I mean, I am running a successful business, so maybe I am good with numbers?* And when I go into a meeting with that new mind-set and change my trigger, I'm more confident and ready for him to tell me to stop spending money.

One trick I like to use is to flip the negative thought in my head to something positive, then look for proof why that positive thought is true.

For example, your negative thought is: I'm not ready to audition for the a cappella group. Switch it to be positive: I *am* ready to audition for the a cappella group because . . .

- I've been practicing for months,
- my pitch is a cross between an angel and Kelly Clarkson, and
- I would make a great addition to Acafellas.

By looking for proof why the positive thought is true, we're making ourselves believe it. We're actually rewiring our brains to be positive.

Get to know the voice in your head as if it's a new neighbor with a sweet pool that you have been dreaming of lounging in every sweltering day. Ask these questions: What makes you happy/sad? When are you weak/strong? What people or scenarios get inside your head? What does your voice tell you in the face of a challenge? In the face of fear? In the face of uncertainty?

And then, just listen.

If we really listen to the things we tell ourselves, sometimes we realize that we're not very nice to ourselves. The most frequent phrase that floats through my head is: *That's not good enough.* No matter if it's in my business, my relationships, or a meal I'm trying to cook, there's this tiny voice that tells me it's not enough. It's the voice that keeps my foot tapping incessantly. But it's also the single thought I'm trying to change because I know it's not true.

So next time a negative thought becomes a barrier to your story, flip it to a positive and look for proof that the positive is true.

2. Personify your voice.

Think of the voice in your head as a person separate from you. You can even give it a different name. Hi, Helga!

According to a study at the University of Michigan, when we separate ourselves from our egos, it reduces anxiety and fear of being evaluated. So instead of talking to yourself with a pronoun like "I" or "me" or "you," we call ourselves by our name. They found that using people's first names in their internal dialogue shifts them away from their self and helps them rise above egocentrism.[9]

In this study, they found that people are better at dealing with other people's problems than they are dealing with their own. Remember the last time a friend came to you with a problem? How did you respond? I'm sure you were kind, compassionate, and calm as you helped walk him or her through it to find a solution. But sometimes when *we* have a problem, we don't talk to ourselves with the same kind of care. We say things like, "How did I let this happen?" or "I'm out of my league here," or "I think I made the wrong choice." Or even worse, we live in the past and say something like, "If only I had . . ."

By treating our internal dialogue like a person or a friend, we can separate ourselves from it. And when we separate ourselves from it, it's easier to get clarity and not let the anxiety of our ego take over.

When people talk to us, we also sometimes have this BS filter where we question what that person is saying. We should be doing the same thing for our own internal dialogue. When we say something negative, we should call ourselves out on it. Call yourself out for being mean to yourself. And sometimes you can be so in tune with the voice in your head that you can call out the BS and link it back to where it stemmed from, perhaps a belief you had as a kid or bad advice a former boss gave you.

But at the end of the day, personifying the voice in your head has one golden rule: Would you talk to yourself the way you talk to a friend? Would you tell your friend that he or she isn't good enough? I hope not, so you shouldn't talk to yourself that way either.

3. Take small actions.

Much of our inner dialogue is shaped by our follow-through. In other words, do we actually *do* the things we say we're going to do in our heads? Like when we tell ourselves we're going to wake up early and go to the gym, but then our alarm goes off and we're like, "No thanks, Helga." But then when we do get out of bed later and we're rushing to work, we feel a slight sting because we didn't follow through on what we said we were going to do. That creates a tone for negative self-talk that could continue throughout the day.

When we cross things off our to-do list, it breeds confidence. Even when we accomplish small things, we feel more confident and able to keep going. When we finish something, our inner dialogue is like, *Heck yeah, sister! What else you got?* Maybe your voice is more soft-spoken than mine, but the girl in my head can be like a personal trainer who's had too much coffee.

My point is, when we accomplish things—even small stuff—we're building a positive inner dialogue. We're putting our self-talk in her happy place. And when she's in her happy place, she thinks about all the other things that are possible.

Completing small actions equals positive self-talk to then do *bigger* actions.

Whether it's doing the laundry or giving your dog a haircut (actually, that's not a small action; I tried it and it takes forever), you're making your inner dialogue happy because you're thinking and then executing. Don't overwhelm yourself by thinking of something *huge* you want to do; just give your inner dialogue the satisfaction of crossing little things off your list. And before you know it, those little things will add up to something huge.

Take, for example, running a mile.

When my sister and I were in elementary school, we were in one of the first-ever Girls on the Run groups. Girls on the Run is a wonderful nonprofit that teaches young girls life skills through running. As a part of the program, you had to do a one-mile run the first day. At the time a mile seemed like the kind of distance planes were invented for. But somewhere between twelve and twenty-three minutes later, I ran my first mile.

After we crossed the finish line, which was actually just a high five from our coach, my sister and I felt on top of the world. We just ran a *whole* mile. The Girls on the Run coach told us in two months we would be running a 5K, which she translated for me as a whopping 3.1 miles.

That seemed like way too much. More like a cross-country trip where you'd go ocean to ocean. But my sister said, "Jess, if we can run one mile, we can totally run three!"

I figured it was the endorphins talking, but it wasn't.

A few months later, we ran a 5K together. After the 5K we eventually ran a 10K. Then after the 10K we ran a half marathon. After the half, my sister wanted us to run a full marathon. I told her the only way I'd do it is if we did the Disney Marathon, so we did.

I definitely loved the pre-race dinner more than I loved the actual race. The night before the marathon when you carb load was one of the best nights of my life (my wedding a close second). My sister told me it was socially acceptable to eat all the carbs my heart desired because I'd burn them off in the race. I heard Lizzie McGuire's song in my head, "This is what dreaaaaams are made of!" We went to a pasta buffet and I was like Joey Chestnut at the Nathan's Hot Dog Eating Contest. Alfredo, marinara, pesto, you name it. We came. We carbed. We conquered.

We survived the marathon and I thought we had officially peaked with our running, but my sister had other plans. After we ran a marathon, my sister ran a forty-mile race, a fifty-mile race, and then a hundred-mile race. Yes, you read that correctly. My sister ran one hundred miles on her own two feet. And she's done it multiple times.

The first time Heather did a hundred-mile race, I had a speaking gig in Pennsylvania so I couldn't be there. But she had a tracking chip on her shoe and an app where I could see her progress. I remember being half deep in a burrito, watching the app from an airport, and saying, "Run, Heather! Keep going!" [Continues eating burrito.]

Her next hundred-miler was in Asheville, North Carolina, and her boyfriend (*hoping* he's her fiancé or husband when this book comes out. C'mon, just do it already! You two were made for each other!) was supposed to be her pacer for the last part. They allow each runner to have a pacer toward the end to keep them on track, because running one hundred miles can make you delirious. Go figure.

I was ready to pull an all-nighter and watch Heather run from the sidelines and drink hot chocolate to stay warm and maybe even whip out my UGG boots from the '90s. But two weeks before the race, Heather called me: "Jess, I need you to be my pacer. Brock can't come."

"Awwwww," I said. "I'm so flattered. I'd love to run the last mile with you!"

I pictured us holding hands, crossing the finish line with cameras flashing, and I put her on my shoulders and everyone's chanting

"Heath-er, Heath-er!" And then everyone compliments me for being so selfless and *such* a supportive sister.

"The pacer has to run the last twenty miles with me," she said.

"Oh, HALE no."

Click.

Okay, I didn't actually hang up on her, but I wanted to. Twenty miles was crazy, and it had been years since I ran the marathon (okay, it had been years since I ran more than five miles). Then she told me that part of my job running the last twenty miles with her would be to make sure she was eating and to have talking points to keep her distracted. These are two things I happen to be very good at, so I agreed.

I opened up my journal and started writing questions to use for the race:

- If you could have the bottom half of any animal, which one would it be and why?
- Which three emojis do you use most? And which one do you wish existed?
- Who would play you in a movie?
- Tell me your thoughts on Bigfoot.
- What three new skills do you want to acquire?
- Team Britney or Christina?
- Let's come up with a movie involving squirrels wearing goggles with superpowers.
- I open my fortune cookie—what does it say?
- If I gave you $5,000 right now, what would you buy me?
- If you could put only one condiment on food for the rest of your life, which condiment would you choose?
- Can you believe you still have seventeen miles to go?
- I'm gonna pop into this Chipotle; do you want chicken or barbacoa? Or are you still eating only soy-based products?

I spent the next two weeks Googling on my phone: *What should I be doing right now if I have to run twenty miles?*

I was traveling a lot for speaking engagements so it was hard to train and get in a routine (or that's what I told myself since I wasn't training). Finally it was the day of the race. The gun went off for Heather at 5:00 a.m. in Asheville. I was in Detroit giving a speech and had the whole audience virtually cheer Heather on during my presentation. After I was done, I ran out to meet my driver and went to the airport. I landed in Asheville at 10:00 p.m. and Heather was still running. I got a few hours of sleep in a random tent with people I didn't know, and she came by the eighty-mile marker early the next morning. We started running.

I'll admit, when I first heard that my sister wanted to run one hundred miles, I questioned how we came from the same gene pool. But during that race and running the last leg with her, I felt like I finally got it.

THE POWER OF POSITIVITY

This wasn't about what her body could do, it was about what her mind told her she could do. And this huge venture of running a one-hundred-mile race started with one small action: running one mile.

I have to believe the initial thought of physically running one hundred miles seems impossible to just about anyone the first time. But from that first mile we ran at Girls on the Run, my sister made her internal voice of encouragement louder and louder in her head. *If I can run this far, what else can I do?*

Of course, her voice could have spoken very differently. Her voice could have told her that it's impossible to run one hundred miles. Her voice could have told her that more people will go to the moon than run one hundred miles. Her voice could have told her to sit down and know her limits. Her voice could have told her that she can't fail sitting on the couch.

Her voice could have listened to all the people (including me) telling her not to do it. But instead her inner dialogue told her to lace up her running shoes and go for it. And that's the power of positivity. It's the single thing that can empower you to do what might seem impossible to others but makes perfect sense to you.

A lot of our goals and dreams can seem like a one-hundred-mile race, something that is so far-fetched why even try? A million-dollar business seemed like that for me. Speaking onstage in front of thousands of people seemed like that for me. Writing this book seemed like that for me.

And there's still one-hundred-mile races I have yet to finish, like having an inspirational Netflix comedy special. But whenever I'm letting the voice in my head make me feel small or tell myself a narrative I don't want to hear, I try to separate myself from my thoughts, call BS on Helga, and replace it with something that serves the story I want to write.

Sometimes it's not about totally silencing the voice in your head (because she can get loud). Instead acknowledge its presence, then slowly push it to the side and give more and more airtime to the good stuff and less and less to the bad. As you do, the negative thoughts will have less and less real estate in your head.

BE YOUR OWN CHEERLEADER

When I was a kid, my parents came to all of my volleyball games. Whenever I'd come off the bench or even touch the ball, I'd hear my dad in the stands yell, "Let's go, *Ekstroooom!*"

I was always so embarrassed. We even have this craziness on film. But now I realize the way my dad embarrassingly and ferociously cheered for me is how I want to cheer for myself. I want my inner dialogue to cheer so loud it embarrasses me. And that's how we should all talk to ourselves when we need a little extra nudge to take that first step.

It's okay to be inwardly cocky and tell yourself you're the best thing since *NOW That's What I Call Music!* Volume 6 (because that's the one that had "Bye Bye Bye" and "Love Don't Cost a Thing" on it). We can't wait for other people to sit in our stands and cheer us on. If we're just waiting to hear someone else's voice in our corner, we're handing over the power of our own confidence and happiness.

In my opinion, the biggest barrier to success is not what we know, where we went to school, how many resources we have, or any of the things we put such high priority on. The biggest barrier to success is our inner dialogue saying it's not our turn. It's turning down the job as a water aerobics instructor or telling ourselves we've already peaked.

As kids (and sometimes as adults) we were always told: Don't gloat. Don't speak too highly of yourself. Don't be too comfortable with your abilities. But now I feel like this advice is misleading. I'm not saying that we should drop into a touchdown dance in our office every time we make a sale. But what if we had an unwavering belief in ourselves? What if we always knew that there was nothing too big to stand in our way? What if we truly believed that against all odds we will always figure it out?

Is that being cocky? Maybe. But is that better than sitting where we are because we don't trust our abilities? Heck, yes.

I was once on a panel where college students could ask those of us in the lineup career advice. One student asked about interviewing techniques, and a panelist responded, "Be prepared, bring something to write with, be inquisitive but not overly confident."

Another panelist disagreed. "Be a little cocky. Try it on. See where it takes you."

I'll admit, I was a little flabbergasted by his response. But now I see his point. With Headbands of Hope, I *had* to be overly confident to make it work because the first step to reaching your goal is telling yourself you can make it.

I'm giving you permission to be a little cocky. Try it on. See where it takes you.

I'm not saying if we just believe in ourselves that everything will work out perfectly, but if we tell ourselves to go for it, the opportunities might be uncertain but at least they're there.

But if we tell ourselves we're not good enough, we know *exactly* what the future will hold because we're currently living in it. Nothing will change.

Optimism requires us to direct our internal dialogue to something greater. We can't manifest a brighter future without good thoughts passing through our neural pathways. Everything wonderful that has been created or achieved had to start with someone who believed it could be better.

In order to believe something better exists, we must train our inner voices to look for it and believe that it's us. Think of it this way: the life we want is waiting on the other side of our thoughts. It's up to you when you're going to join it.

Take It or Leave It

Start to recognize some of the daily thoughts that go through your head and write them down. Then for each one, ask yourself: *Is this story helping me get to where I want to go?*

If yes: How can we build more truth? For example, if the thought is: *I'd make a really good dog walker.* And you want to be more active, out in the community, making some more cash, then keep building positivity off of this thought like: *And I could do it before I go to work. I could ask my friends to give me testimonials.*

If no: How can we change the dialogue? For example, if the thought is: *I'd make a really bad dog walker.* And you want to be more active, out in the community, making some more cash, then change the dialogue by looking for ways that this thought *isn't* true: *Actually, my neighbor's dog loves me and they're always asking me to walk her. I have some extra time in the evenings when I could walk dogs just to get started.*

OUR TOUGHER EXPERIENCES TEND TO *strip* US FROM ALL THE THINGS THAT DON'T REALLY *matter* AND ADJUST OUR *focus* ON WHAT DOES.

Twelve

THE STRUGGLE IS WORTH IT

Life is like photography. You need
the negatives to develop.
—ZIAD K. ABDELNOUR

When I was a kid, my mom knew I was about to hit puberty, not because I was developing but because of an abrupt mood change. I was always the happiest kid. I never really got upset or cried unless someone stole my food. But one day, out of the blue, I started crying and ran to my room. My mom followed me upstairs and looked at me with confusion.

"What's wrong?" she said, knowing this was truly out of character for me.

"Mom! I have sadness!" I explained, motioning down my arms where, apparently, I was feeling sadness like I was breaking out from poison ivy.

"I don't know where it's coming from!" Again talking about sadness like I brushed against a bush, got a rash, and needed a cream.

As if on cue, my mom went to her room and pulled out American Girl's *The Care and Keeping of You*, which is basically a playbook for puberty. She handed me the book and started explaining what was happening to me. I looked at the book in my hands and felt like I was getting served.

"You mean you're telling me this happens every month?"

Sure enough, about a week later I was hiding in a hoodie while going down the feminine product aisle with my mom seeing words like *comfort, pearl, radiant, sport,* and *flow.*

Because being anything less than Happy Jess was out of character for me as a kid, my mom knew exactly what was happening when I was upset for no particular reason. However, periods aside, even as I started to get older, I felt like I had to stay true to my Happy Jess reputation. I could have very well given this reputation to myself, but I felt like anything less than a ray of sunshine was weakness. Most of the time I was genuinely very happy, but if I was upset or sad about something, I'd steamroll right through it like a Major League Baseball player jumping into the stands to make a catch.

So when it came to my business, I took the same approach: Smile for the camera. Everything's always fine and dandy. Just keep swimming.

When I was in this be-happy-all-the-time phase, I got the sweetest email from a teenage girl who had cancer. She did YouTube videos on beauty and fashion, and she wanted to see if I'd send her some headbands for her YouTube channel. I sent her a huge basket of products and loved watching her review them on camera:

"I love this one because it ties in the back and the ribbon makes me feel like I have a ponytail!"
"This one is super soft on my bald head."
"They all are just so cute—you can't even choose a favorite!"

After watching the video, I sent it out on social media and to friends and family. I was so impressed with her confidence and poise being a young teen with cancer and starting her YouTube channel. I followed her on social media and we kept in touch, commenting and supporting each other.

Then one day I was scrolling on Instagram and saw a message from her account. Her family wrote a post that she had passed away, and they wanted to thank everyone for the love and support over the years.

I squinted my eyes, reading it again and again. It didn't feel real.

Even though I was fully aware that she had cancer, I never let myself think past that. I had never met her in person, but I felt like I knew her. I could picture her starting her own beauty empire and using her story of overcoming cancer as a part of her brand. It never even crossed my mind that her story would go differently because I didn't let my mind go there.

IT'S OKAY TO NOT BE OKAY

I was still in school at the time, and I remember finding the closest bathroom and sitting in a stall, watching her video on repeat and crying. Even though I was blindsided and maybe shouldn't have been, that experience taught me it's *okay* to not be okay.

Our lives aren't meant to be lived at the highest volume all the time. It's hard to make that distinction because oftentimes we see only the good in other people's lives so we feel like all of our moments have to match what we see. But feeling the depth in these pockets of life where we experience pain is not showing weakness; it shows that we're brave enough to face these emotions for what they are and hopefully use them to inspire something more.

I was once talking to a pediatric oncology doctor and he said to me, "The moment one of my patients becomes 'just another patient,' it's time for me to retire."

I was so upset with this girl's passing, but I also wanted to keep going in her memory. I sent a donation of headbands in her name to the hospital where she was treated and shared her video with beauty bloggers we worked with to show how great she was.

SITTING IN THE DARK

Eventually her memory in my heart went from a sting to a warmth. The moments when we're not okay are adding more color and depth to our life's palette. By allowing ourselves to feel the spectrum of emotions and owning when we are in pain, we give ourselves the gift of being more grateful in the light and more resilient and determined in the dark.

Because here's an interesting difference I've found between living in the light and the dark: When we're in the light, why leave? Everything is fine here. But when we're in the dark, that's when we scramble. That's when we act. That's when we become resourceful. That's when we appreciate any flicker of good in our life. That's when we move, because anything is better than here.

So as weird as it sounds, the darkness is necessary for growth. We move when we're trying to fix something. And in order to fix something, it has to be broken. Nonprofits and foundations are not started to make happy people happier; they exist to bring light to the dark.

For example, think about the important work being done by the following foundations:

- **Joyful Heart**: Transforming society's response to sexual assault, domestic violence, and child abuse; supporting survivors' healing; and ending this violence forever.
- **Human Rights Campaign**: Creating a world where LGBTQ people are ensured of their equal rights so they can be open, honest, and safe at home, at work, and in the community.
- **Stop Bullying Now**: Raising money for school districts around the country to address and eliminate the ongoing bullying problem, which is causing much mental and physical harm, even death.

Courageous individuals started those foundations out of the darkness. And in order for us to be that change too, we have to be brave enough to see the darkness as an opportunity to bring good instead of an excuse to pull back.

SEE THE GOOD

I first met my flower girl when she was around seven years old at North Carolina Children's Hospital. I had just started Headbands of Hope, so I was still nervous going into hospitals, but Embree immediately put me at ease. When I walked into her room, she was wearing a bright-colored outfit and welcomed me like we were entering her treehouse, not her hospital room.

I remember asking her, "What do you like to do for fun?"

Without skipping a beat, she replied, "I like doing cartwheels around my house and handstands up against my wall."

At that moment, I knew we were going to get along. She picked out a soft pink headband, and we took pictures and laughed until it was time to go.

About a year later, I was delivering headbands to a camp for kids with illnesses and I heard a high-pitched, "*Jess!*"

I turned around and I saw Embree running toward me at full speed, wearing her soft pink headband she had picked out in the hospital a year ago. She introduced me to her friends in her cabin and said, "This is my friend, Jess. She gave me this headband in the hospital, and she has headbands for you too."

Embree asked me to stay a little longer so she could go back to her cabin and give me a magnet she made. The magnet said, "We make a living by what we get, but we make a life by what we give." I still have that magnet on my fridge.

Over the years, I kept in touch with Embree and her mom. It was really heartbreaking when she was cancer free then relapsed shortly after. But Embree handled it like a champ, saying, "Cancer better run!" and "This cancer doesn't know who it's messing with."

When she was well enough, I'd pick Embree up and we'd take a walk in the park or go get smoothies. My favorite day was when I brought over tie-dye stuff and our tie-dyed shirts turned out *awful*, but we still wore them. We even bought ugly Christmas sweaters and did a photoshoot and sent out a holiday card together one year.

One day I picked her up and took her to a new lunch spot that had just opened. At this point, Embree had lost her hair again. She had her port for chemotherapy clipped onto her shorts. But no matter how she was feeling, she always wore something fashionable (and a headband, of course).

We were at the restaurant eating our food, talking about middle school and celebrity gossip. A waiter came by and said, "Would you like to try some of our new cookies?"

"Sure!" we both shouted, maybe a little too quickly.

About ten minutes later, a different waiter came by and said, "We made a little too much of this smoothie, would you guys like the extra?"

Of course! Then we drank the pink smoothie, which tasted even better when it was free.

To cap off the lunch, another waiter walked by with two small cups of wellness shots and asked if we wanted them.

"Absolutely!" Embree shouted.

As he walked away, Embree looked at me, holding the energy shot in one hand and smoothing the top of her head with the other, and with a wink said, "Thanks, cancer."

I cracked up with how comfortable she was talking about her cancer and knowing it was probably the reason we kept getting free stuff. Embree was choosing to see the good in her disease. She even created the acronym TCJ, which stands for "tasteful cancer jokes." Whenever she makes fun of her cancer, she goes, "It's okay, it's just a TCJ."

When I got married I asked Embree to be my flower girl. She was so excited and immediately started talking about dresses and what headband she would wear. She ended up bringing three headbands and interchanged them throughout the night.

We had an open mic at our rehearsal dinner so anyone could come up and say a few words about Jake and me. And when I say anyone, I mean anyone—except for my grandpa, because he's a high risk for saying something *wildly* inappropriate. But other than that, it was fair game.

Some of my best friends from college made a remix rap to the *Fresh Prince of Bel-Air* song, some family members told embarrassing stories, and staff from Headbands of Hope shared some fun memories. The night went on and I thought the speeches were over. Then I heard a small voice come over the speakers, "Hello? Is this thing on?"

Everyone turned their heads to see Embree at the top of the stairs with the microphone, overlooking the rehearsal dinner. I couldn't believe it—she was in middle school and about to improvise a speech in public! "Hi! I'm Embree. I met Jess when I was in the hospital when I had cancer for the first time. I remember I thought she was so fun and we've been friends ever since."

She shared memories of us over the years, said some TCJs, and then ended the speech with, "Oh, and Jake, I'm sure you're great too." There wasn't a dry eye at the rehearsal dinner. The next day I walked down the aisle and was so thrilled to see Embree's face in the lineup of everyone I love. When I watched the ceremony video later, I saw that after she made it down the aisle tossing flowers, she dabbed to the crowd. That's my girl.

Today Embree is still being treated for cancer. I'm typing this chapter in a coffee shop around the corner from the hospital, waiting for her to get out of surgery. I'm sure she has her moments when she's frustrated that she can't go to see her friends or be in the school play. But overall, her positivity makes me want to see the good, even in the bad.

A few weeks ago Embree was showing me the journal she created, and on one of the pages she wrote a quote by Helen Keller, "Keep your face to the sun and you cannot see the shadows. It's what the sunflowers do."

To me, Embree chooses to face the sun even when times are hard.

On the next page she wrote, "Shake it like a polaroid picture." It's called balance.

Embree is a role model for how we should approach tough times in our lives. She feels what she feels when she feels it. Sometimes that's anger, frustration, and sadness. But she never lets those emotions write her narrative. That's what optimistic people do. They feel all emotions, but they choose to come back to positivity and hope in due time. Embree is too busy living a wonderful life and finding reasons to laugh, even if it's about her illness, to sit too long in the darkness of cancer. She feels the spectrum of emotions without letting the negatives write her story.

WHERE WE'RE BUILT

At Headbands of Hope, we have a program called Headband Heroes, where people volunteer to be a brand ambassador for us. Most of our heroes are college women, but not all of them. One of our heroes, Rachel, was a college student in Washington who also had cancer. She had heard about Headbands of Hope through her hospital and applied to be a Headband Hero, and of course she was accepted with open arms.

Rachel and I chatted over email, and we decided to do a story on her for our newsletter and social media. We shipped headbands out to her so she could do a photo shoot with them, and she wrote a blog about what it's like having cancer and why the headbands are so meaningful. She was always in high spirits and willing to use her story for the greater good.

About a year later, I got an email from her mom:

Jess,

My name is Mary and I'm Rachel's mom. After her passing, we wanted to reach out to the organizations she loved most and see how we can support them. Headbands of Hope was her favorite and we'd love to support it. Let us know if this is possible.

Mary

It was another moment when I felt like I had lost a friend. I had never met her in person, but our email and social media exchanges were enough for me to realize she was someone special. About a month later I flew out to Seattle and met up with her mom. Together we delivered headbands to Mary Bridge Children's Hospital where Rachel was treated. Her mom was telling me how Rachel's spirit animal was a ladybug. On her first day of chemotherapy, there was a ladybug inside her treatment room, which is unheard of. We made ladybug headbands for Rachel, and whenever a ladybug lands on me, I think of her.

My experiences with children with cancer have not been all hearts and flower crowns and ladybugs. It can be excruciatingly tough, but I know whatever I'm feeling, it's worse for the patients and their families. But these moments are where we're built. Our tougher experiences tend to strip us of all the things that don't really matter and adjust our focus on what does.

There were moments when I was living in a constant state of dusk. I never really let myself see too much darkness or too much light; I was just protecting myself by staying neutral. But looking back, some of the most transformative moments in my life were the hardest. And whenever we want to do something big or create change, we're going to encounter hardships. We might see or experience things that make us uncomfortable. But we first have to recognize that seeing the bad is also seeing the truth, even if it's hard.

On one hand, it might be easier to build a wall in front of anything that causes us pain or discomfort. On the other hand, experiencing pain and discomfort can be the starting point for action. The times when we really go for it are typically the times when we're experiencing something bad:

- You have a health scare, so you start exercising.
- You need more money, so you pick up some side-hustles.
- You see animals in need, so you rescue a dog.
- You go through a breakup and you start practicing meditation, yoga, and other mindfulness practices.

- Someone you love passes, so you start a foundation in his or her memory.
- You're bored and unhappy, so you book a one-way ticket across the country and don't look back.

When everything is going smoothly, you don't really think about shaking it up. Sometimes it takes the darkness and discomfort to mobilize us to find the light.

Optimism has the connotation of being *all* about happiness. But truly, optimism is most important when things are tough. It's okay to recognize moments for what they are: sad, disappointing, tough, or hard. We don't have to hypnotize ourselves to feel happy all the time, especially when an experience warrants a negative emotion. If we brush over the tough times, we're not giving them the opportunity to shape us. And when we allow them to shape us, that's when we can really bring good to this world. We have to let the dark moments be the reason why we bring the light.

I like to classify these tough times as a moment or a movement. Is it just a fleeting moment that threw you off your game for a beat? Or does the tough time spark a movement to work toward something better? The #MeToo movement started with moments of bravery that became a massive movement. The "Ice Bucket Challenge" started with a few video clips that became a cultural fund-raising phenomenon. My company started with a moment where I saw that kids liked to wear headbands during cancer treatment, and I am proud to say that our headbands have been passed out in every children's hospital in the country.

A moment or a movement. The choice is yours.

Take It or Leave It

Sit in the dark. I don't mean literally in a dark room, but the next time you come across something sad or uncomfortable, even if it's a commercial for the SPCA, sit with it for a minute. If you're triggered by something that means it's meaningful to you. So instead of breezing past it to get back to happy, what could you do to help?

FULFILLMENT IS NOT A *destination* WE REACH THROUGH ACHIEVEMENTS, IT'S A *choice* ON HOW WE LIVE OUR LIVES *right now.*

#chasingthebrightside

Thirteen

ALIGNMENT OVER ATTENTION

*Change the way you look at things and
the things you look at change.*
—WAYNE DYER

One time I got an email from a huge magazine (more than eight million copies are issued around the world every month). They said they'd like me to enter their contest to be their Woman of the Year. And in the email they said: "The winner of the competition will be on the cover of our October issue."

After that sentence, I was in. I was picturing myself standing in the grocery store line and seeing myself on the cover of a *magazine*. What would I wear? What would the issue say? What would everyone say who sees me on this cover? How many copies could I request for free and send them out as Christmas gifts? I had to win this.

I responded that I was in. A few weeks later they flew me and four other finalists to New York City to do photo shoots for the print issue and video for their online site. The other women in the competition were incredible, and I still keep in touch with them.

After the photo shoot, the magazine released the competition to the public to vote for a month. It was the last thing I'd think about when I went to bed and the first thing I'd think of when I woke up. My husband was sending out the voting link to his office, telling people behind the counter at the pharmacy, and mentioning it to everyone he ever knew. My grandpa was teaching all his elderly friends how to get on the internet and vote. My mom would tell every cashier or person she came in contact with to vote for me. I was appreciative, but it solidified my lifelong belief that I will *never* go into politics.

Then I got the email.

Jess,

We are pleased to tell you that you have been selected as our Woman of the Year. Please sign the attached forms and we'll be in touch for further details.

I quickly screenshotted the email and forwarded it to my family, who went *nuts*. But for me, it was a momentary rush and then nothing. I just kept thinking: *So what happens next? How can I leverage this? When's the cover shoot?*

Time passed, and I was getting suspicious about this whole "cover shoot." I sent them an email asking when the shoot would be. They responded a few days later.

We regret to inform you that our sponsorship for the cover shoot fell through, so the winner will not be featured on the cover.

And there it was. No cover shoot.

But for some reason this didn't shock me. It actually, for some crazy reason, made sense. I'd had a feeling the whole time I was chasing this that something didn't feel right. It's like when you're throwing spices into a pot to make a soup and deep down you really think it's going to taste like crap but you keep following the recipe because you're already committed. Or you're watching a Hallmark Christmas movie you know is awful but you're too invested to see if the girl chooses the hometown guy over the businessman and finally understands the "true meaning of Christmas."

ALIGNMENT VS. ATTENTION

I didn't know it at the time, but this sinking feeling in my stomach was the feeling of being out of alignment. Alignment is our inner applause. Alignment is the moment where we know our efforts and work are pointing to something bigger and greater than ourselves. We can connect the dots from the actions we took to why they matter in a bigger picture. Our inner applause is that "heck, yes" feeling we get when we know we're making a difference in a way that is meaningful to us; that feeling when you pass by a mirror and you didn't even realize you were smiling.

But alignment is something that can't be seen, it can only be felt. For that reason, sometimes it gets blurry when we try to differentiate our alignment from our attention.

Attention is the outer applause: the accolades, the likes, the recognition, the high fives. . . the magazine cover. And here's the thing: the accolades are fine. I'm not saying that you should swat away a trophy or cross out any titles with a Sharpie. Everyone deserves a pat on the back every now and then. But we can celebrate the accolades and high fives along the way without making them the driving force behind our happiness and fulfillment.

When we equate getting accolades with happiness and success, we give them too much airtime in our heads. In doing so we become more and more focused on getting recognition and awards and less and less concerned with the true meaning behind why we do what we do. We must continuously find ways to realign ourselves to the why behind our work. When accolades do come, you can be grateful but treat them as if you've seen a shooting star: beautiful, unexpected, but also temporary. Enjoy the moment, then get back to doing work that lights your spirit.

CONDITIONED FOR ATTENTION

Trust me, you're talking to the former queen of accolades.

I started Headbands of Hope to help kids with cancer. As stupid as this sounds, I honestly didn't even realize that there was going to be potential for recognition in that. It was a reaction to a need rather than a feather in my cap (or on my headband) that I wanted applause for. But I read something in Amy Poehler's book, *Yes Please*, that resonated with me. She talked about how she never wanted any of the awards. She was perfectly fine without them. But once you're told you're in the running for one, your whole mind shifts. Once it's dangled in front of you, you feel like you *have* to have it, like a horse trotting toward a carrot. (Do horses even like carrots?) Once you know it's a possibility—when it wasn't even a twinkle in your eye before—then it *has* to be you.

And that's what it was for me. I really didn't care about the awards or the attention in the beginning because it wasn't my motive. But once I started getting them, it was like a dog being rewarded a treat for the first time. I would sit, stay, roll over, shake, and chase a squirrel to Mexico until someone gave me a treat again. I was hungry for headlines.

That's exactly what happens when we post on social media and get likes or do something and get rewarded. We become conditioned for attention. We get stuck in the trap of performing for something other than ourselves.

Of course I realize that social media can be just a trophy shelf for accolades, achievements, and attention. Who can make the most noise, have the most impressive bio, or snap the photo with the most likes. When you're swimming in that, you feel like that's the metric. You feel your worth and value are dependent upon the attention you receive from others. And the more accolades and tangible achievements you earn, the more attention you get. At least that was my formula. I started to put perception over purpose.

A few years into my business, I went to the hospital and met a girl named Taylor who was fifteen years old, and we picked out an awesome purple and green flower headband that looked so great on her. She told me she was feeling kind of down in the dumps because she was seeing on social media that all of her friends were going to prom and getting asked out in these huge romantic gestures or prom dress shopping with their moms. Prom was not in the cards for her because she couldn't leave the hospital.

I told her I was going to a trade show in Atlanta that week, but when I got back I'd come back to the hospital and we'd have our own prom. We'd get dressed up, take pictures, and listen to music. She was super excited and added me on Facebook so we could chat about the details.

A few days later I was leaving for Atlanta and realized the tags I had ordered to go along with our headbands for the trade show still had not arrived. I was already wound up enough about how much money I was spending on this trade show that these missing tags totally set me off. They were lost in the mail and didn't seem like they were going to get there in time. I got to Atlanta and called the tag company to see if they could overnight a new order of tags directly to the show. They said they couldn't, and I proceeded to tell them that they were ruining my business, one tag at a time.

As I was on the phone with this tag company, I got a call-waiting notification from an unknown number.

I rolled my eyes, thinking it was just another cold call from someone trying to sell me business insurance, and I switched over the line with a quick, "This is Jess."

"Hi, Jess," a soft, gentle voice responded. "This is Taylor's mom, from the hospital."

I immediately switched gears and ran to a corner to find a quiet space.

"Hi!" I said, way more cheerfully than I originally answered the phone. "How are you? How's Taylor?"

"Well," she said softly. "That's why I'm calling. Taylor passed away last night, and I wanted to see if we could get those same purple and green headbands you gave her for every female in our family to wear to her service."

I couldn't find the words to respond.

"You see," she continued, "Taylor really loved that headband. She never took it off since you gave it to her. She kept talking about you and how you two were going to have a prom together, and you just made her so happy her last few days of life. We thought Taylor would love it if we all wore that same headband in her memory."

I don't remember what I said back. I do remember that we got her family the purple and green headbands.

But I remember standing there in the corner of this trade show building with carts and people running around frantically, and all of a sudden it fell silent to me. I remember everything seemed really bright and I heard a loud ringing in my right ear. It was as if my whole life had been moving in fast forward and someone hit the Pause button for me. A button I should have hit myself a long time ago.

I felt the weight of this anchor pull me back down to feel my feet on the ground. I hadn't realized how far I had been drifting. Why did I start all of this in the first place? It wasn't to be on the cover of a magazine or be the best booth at a trade show. It was to serve kids with illnesses and their families.

MISDIAGNOSING YOUR NEEDS

That moment, standing in the corner of that trade show, was when I discovered the disconnect between attention and alignment.

My focus was more on attention from the public and less on the alignment of my mission. I was on a hamster wheel, chasing things that would never truly fulfill me. It's like when you think you're hungry but you're actually thirsty, but you keep eating, waiting for it to quench the feeling, but it never does. You're misdiagnosing your needs.

I thought that the attention meant success. But attention and success are not codependent. You can have success without the attention. And you can have the attention without the success.

In the early days of Headbands of Hope, I felt so close to everything. Everything was so new and so fresh and it was so easy to see how everything I did connected to a beautiful and meaningful result of kids with cancer getting headbands. Every win (even the small ones) felt like I was accepting an Oscar. Even though I was broke and chasing anything shiny, I felt so connected to what I was doing because I was involved with everything. And when you're starting from the bottom, anything remotely above bottom feels like you're soaring.

I felt like I was Oprah, skipping around and giving unsolicited advice to people that "if they truly cared about what they were doing, then work wouldn't feel like work." I had it all figured out.

But as the years went on and the business expanded, things started to feel heavier.

Staff came on board. Contracts got bigger. Overhead got more expensive. Plans got longer. Warehouses got bigger. Inboxes got messier. Decisions were heavier. And the bigger the tree that Headbands of Hope grew to be, the farther away I got from the roots. I was always so focused on what was next and what would make us (and me) look good. I started to get more concerned with what people would say than how it made me feel. I cared more about what other people believed *about* me rather than my belief *in* me and my mission.

I kept stocking up on attention: TV shows, celebrities, press, awards, and so on. It was like filling a barrel with water when it had a leak in the bottom that I couldn't see. I kept filling and filling but it would never be full.

I was anxious and stressed all the time. Nothing was ever good enough and there was always something *just* out of my reach. Like if I could just get on this 30 Under 30 list, then I'll be set. Or if I could just hit this revenue number, I'll feel like a successful business woman.

WHAT ARE YOU CHASING?

Don't get me wrong, I think it's great to have goals and clear dreams you're marching toward, but I always felt like everything I ever wanted was just one more milestone away from where I was standing.

It was like standing on the street and seeing a cupcake shop on the other side. Then when you get to the cupcake shop, now you see an ice cream parlor another block away and you want that too. And it keeps going and going and you're never satisfied and then you wonder one day why your pants don't fit anymore.

Things started happening. I started getting the ice cream and the cupcakes. Celebrities wore our headbands, stores were picking us up, and I was featured in articles and magazines. But it felt like interval training without the endorphins at the end: it was a hit and then nothing. The thing I would be chasing for months would arrive and I'd feel nothing. It's like ordering a dress online and it looks *so* good in the pictures, and then it arrives and the plastic bag it came in would be more appealing than the dress.

When we chase attention and it arrives, we usually breeze right past it because we're looking at the next accolade. But when we chase alignment and we feel lit, it will be more powerful than all of your headlines combined. However, if our focus is on the accolades, we'll miss the feeling of alignment because it's hard to see things we're not looking for.

As a speaker it's easy to want to be on the big stage with the lights and the thousands of people roaring in the audience. I've had those gigs with the thirty-person tech crew, the Britney Spears mic, the HD video, and the long line for pictures after. Heck, I've been on a stage with a fake lion and smoke coming up from the sides. But all it takes is that one letter from an attendee saying I changed the way they think to make me feel aligned, and sometimes that's from a small group of thirty people.

Meaningful moments do not need to be validated with likes and comments. They just need to be felt with purpose and passion.

After Taylor's passing, Headbands of Hope created an event at the children's hospital for kids like Taylor to have the prom night they deserve. With the help of other wonderful childhood cancer organizations like Meg's Smile Foundation, The Monday Life, and ATLAS, we transformed the hospital lobby into a prom night with the theme of "Around the

World." There was a dance floor, a DJ, and food stations from different countries. And of course, a make-your-own-headband station.

I watched the kids arrive with their picture-taking parents wearing sparkly dresses and tuxedos and corsages. I danced the night away with the patients as my husband worked the flower crown station and made no fewer than one hundred flower crowns that night. He's surprisingly good at making flower crowns, and I'm sure he'll be thrilled that I let the world know that.

Because of Taylor's story, I now try to check in and ask myself this question: *The thing that I'm chasing right now, if I got it and no one else knew about it, would it still be meaningful to me?*

The magazine cover: no, I wouldn't care.

The children's hospital prom: yes. Absolutely, yes.

If what you're chasing is only validated by the likes of others, then stop chasing it. But if what you're chasing is something that is meaningful to you without the attention, then go for it at full speed.

So let me ask you a question: When the likes go away and the applause falls silent, is what you're doing right now still meaningful to you? If your next point of impact did not get a like, a retweet, a share, some followers, or a pat on the back, would you still go through with it simply because it mattered? Do you really think that one more award will make you feel fulfilled?

Think about the last time you felt really good about something. For me, it's my time spent in the hospitals interacting with patients. Or when I see a woman post in the Mic Drop Workshop Facebook community that she got her first speaking engagement. I don't have to post about it to know that it's something I'm supposed to be doing.

Getting figuratively slapped in the face by the women's magazine a few years ago made me realize I was caught up chasing attention rather than recalling my alignment. When we're led by optimism, it's pretty easy to feel aligned in the beginning of a venture. Everything is new and fresh and your intentions are pretty clear because you're running off the energy of a raw idea. But then as we start to walk further and further down the path of making our idea a reality, our vision can get blurry. We start to see signs for accolades and other shiny things that can cause us to run off the road and chase something that doesn't really matter.

FULFILLMENT IS A CHOICE

Here's the thing, we usually see fulfillment as a destination, not a choice. Once we get XYZ award or cross ABC milestone, we'll reach fulfillment. But that reasoning is where we're misled and that's why we'll always feel like we came up short whenever we reach those accolades.

Fulfillment is not a destination we reach through achievements, it's a choice on how we live our lives right now. Fulfillment is saying that we care more about what our lives mean than how they look. If that's the case, we don't need to wait for any metric to start living fulfilled lives, we can do that right now. If fulfillment isn't a finish line, then we can simultaneously be fulfilled and driven.

Think about people like Tom Brady, the first player in history to have six Super Bowl wins (if you're a Patriots fan or not, this point is still valid). Do you think he really needs one more Super Bowl ring to feel successful or fulfilled? Probably not. But he keeps playing because he loves the game. He's focused on being better at something that he loves. And when you're driven by a true passion instead of the accolades, that's when you perform at your best.

So instead of stopping what we're doing, sometimes we just need to change the lens through which we see our efforts. Because changing the way we see it can change the way we approach it. Instead of chasing the Super Bowl ring, focus on your love for the game.

I can confidently assume that no one is on their deathbed wishing they got more likes. And our lives don't have to be a tug-of-war between passion and paycheck. We can find our own unique ways to be fulfilled in the life that's right in front of us.

Because success is not what it looks like to others, it's what it feels like to you.

Take It or Leave It

Social media can be great, but it can also be the gasoline for attention. Try taking a cleanse, whether that's a day, a weekend, a week, or even a month. Delete the app from your phone and see how you feel and if you do anything differently when you're not pressured to display your life.

WE CAN SEE OUR *future* IN TWO WAYS: A SCARY MESS OF *uncontrollable* EXPERIENCES OR *plentiful* OPPORTUNITIES TO WRITE OUR OWN STORIES.

#chasingthebrightside

Fourteen

ACTIVATE YOUR PURPOSE

We will never have a perfect world, but it's not
romantic or naive to work toward a better one.
—STEVEN PINKER, PRINTED ON MY
BAG OF CHIPS AT CHIPOTLE

The first time we were on *Good Morning America*, we received more orders in a day than we did our first year of business, which felt pretty freaking good. Our warehouse needed backup getting all the orders out in time, so the whole team got together and showed up at the break of dawn in workout clothes, wearing extra deodorant, and in our headbands of course.

We had a whole system going: there were the chasers who got the correct headbands, the packers who wrapped them up, and the orderers who shouted what was in the order like they were working at McDonald's: "We got one teal baby turban, a gray striped knotted, a scrunchie pack, and a peace clip with three gift bags! Order up!"

We ordered a platter of chicken fingers delivered to the warehouse that we shoved in our mouths during five-minute breaks while we drank gallons of coffee. We blasted Beyoncé on Spotify and came up with our own code words for shouting orders. We'd gotten to the warehouse before the sun rose and it was dark when we left. Our fingers were literally blistered from opening boxes, peeling labels, and affixing tape. But our hearts were full knowing whom we just reached: the millions of people who now knew our name, the thousands of orders on their way to their new homes, and the hundreds of hospitals that were about to get boxes of headbands for their patients.

I sent massage gift cards to the team to get our sore muscles worked out from all the labor we just did, and we all relished in the warm emails we received from everyone, from new customers who received their headbands to hospital staff who couldn't wait to distribute these gifts.

When I dreamed of being a business owner, my vision was definitely not being in a warehouse all day stuffing orders. But I was thrilled to do it because I knew what it meant. Our operations needed my help because the business model was working too well.

MORE THAN JUST *HUSTLE*

You see, when we're triggered by something meaningful, we can't help but roll up our sleeves and put in the work. It's incredible all the work we can do when we're captivated by a greater calling. However, a lot of the language we're fed around working hard is just focused on the hustle, not the trigger.

Raise your hand if you've read something like this:

- The dream is free but the hustle is sold separately.
- Go hard or go home.
- Hustle until you no longer have to introduce yourself.
- Success is never owned, it's rented. And the rent is due every day.
- Hustle in silence and let your success make the noise.
- Good things happen to those who hustle.

We can wake up every day and crank out one hundred push-ups while our raw egg and protein powder is mixing in the blender, but at the end of the day we're still hit with this reality that not a lot of people talk about. It's not sexy to talk about but it's the truth: the hustle doesn't last by itself.

Let me say that a little louder for the folks in the back.

The hustle doesn't last by itself!

We can't just will ourselves to work hard every day. Because willpower, believe it or not, is more like an emotion than it is like gas in the tank. According to the *Harvard Business Review*, willpower is similar to being happy or sad.[10] Willpower is a *feeling* that's triggered by an event that, therefore, influences our actions, like:

- Whether we power up our computer on a plane and choose to work on an article or play solitaire.
- Whether we get off of work and go straight to the gym or go home and watch *The Great British Baking Show*.
- Whether we wake up a few hours early before our normal alarm and work on our side hustle or say we don't have enough time in the day to start it.

If willpower is a feeling, then we need something that triggers that feeling. If we just stand there and try to will ourselves to lose weight or put in the extra hours with nothing powering that request, we might get a slight kick but it won't last. But if we connect these requests to a reason, then that emotion of willpower will be stronger and will produce more organic hustle.

Organic hustle is when you're making strides without begging your mind and your body to follow. It's posting up at a coffee shop on a Sunday working on your side hustle before you have to go back to your full-time job the next day. It's waking up for the 5:00 a.m. boot camp class without wanting to run your head into the wall. Organic hustle is making time for the things you care about and always finding it within you to perform, because it matters.

You know your hustle isn't organic when you feel distracted, forced, or depleted of energy. It's like when you're on your computer trying to work on a project and you keep clicking over to Facebook or Googling videos of dogs that act like cats. But according to the study on willpower in the *Harvard Business Review*, these distracted "feelings are our bodies' way of conveying information that our conscious minds might miss."[11] Whether we're feeling organic hustle kick in or we're clicking over to Facebook, we should listen to it as a source of insight, the same way we listen to things that make us happy or sad.

If a trigger to sadness is dropping our ice cream cone and a trigger to happiness is getting a new ice cream cone, what is a trigger to the feeling of willpower?

What is it that can make us feel like we can do anything?

PURPOSE = WILLPOWER TRIGGER

When I got the idea for Headbands of Hope, I didn't force myself out of bed early every morning to work on this business idea. I got up happily. In fact, I looked forward to it. Why?

Because I knew my efforts were pointing to something bigger than myself.

And in a way, that's my definition of purpose. Purpose at its core is the reason for which something is done or created or for which something exists.[12] So in that moment working on building Headbands of Hope, I knew the reason why this mattered. I knew that all of these small efforts were building something big that was going to help people. I knew that this not only *could* work, it *had* to work because I was solving a problem.

In other words, I was captivated by purpose.

When we're captivated by purpose, our efforts don't feel like chores because it's more fulfilling to do things that matter to us. And when we feel fulfilled, we enjoy our jobs and, therefore, are willing to work harder at them.

For example, when I worked at Disney World, I met two other interns who were both custodians in the parks. One of them absolutely loathed her job and said she just picked up trash and it was dirty and she wanted to go home.

The other custodian who had the *exact* same job thought that he had the best job ever. He would greet guests as they walked in the park, he'd help them plan their day, he'd stop by the office and pick up FastPasses and hand them out to kids, and he was helping keep a park clean so the guests could have a better experience.

These two people had the exact same assigned work: their contracts were the same, the list of tasks they were expected to do were the same. The difference was one saw trash and the other created purpose. Purpose is not assigned to us, it is created by us.

BUT WHAT'S MY PURPOSE?

If the core definition of purpose points to why we exist, that doesn't make it so easy to say, "Oh, yes! I exist because . . ."

But when people talk about purpose and where they feel fulfilled, it's never because they've done something great for themselves; it's always because something they did affected others in a positive way.

So one thread of purpose is "action that helps others."

But we can probably think of lots of things to do to help others that we don't classify as our purpose. So the second thread of purpose is "doing something that you love to do."

What is something you do that brings you joy? Again, a big question but I think a little less daunting than "Why do we exist?" Nevertheless, the hybrid of finding something you love to do that also impacts people in a positive way is your purpose.

I've discovered that my purpose is to give people confidence in who they are now and what they want to do in the future. I love making people feel like they're perfect as they are and they can do anything they want in their one life. And for me, I can do that by building different ventures that accomplish this mission.

Headbands of Hope aims to make kids feel confident with a simple accessory. Mic Drop Workshop is an online course and community to give women the tools to be confident onstage and become professional speakers. My speeches always aim to make my audience feel confident through my storytelling. And the aim of this book is to make you feel confident to write a good story.

UNRAVEL YOUR PAST

I believe one of the best ways to explore what matters to you is to look back to early in your life and think about what mattered to you then. Because the core of what mattered to you then might not be far off from what matters to you now, just in a different shape.

Think about why those moments mattered to you so much:

- Did you want to be a teacher when you were a kid? What is it teachers do for their students that you want to do for other humans?
- How about that time you went to the hibachi restaurant for the first time and they cooked in front of you? Or when Grandma taught you how to make her famous sweet potato pie? Is that when you realized you could warm people's hearts through their stomachs?
- Did you ever get sick or go to the hospital when you were younger? How did those nurses make you feel? Could you recreate that feeling for someone? How about the doctors? What did they do that was cool and impactful, and how could you do it?
- Remember your uncle who loved fast cars and you always wanted to ride with on family trips or just to the store and back? Where can you find a way to create that same rush sensation in others?

- When you binge-watched *Dirty Jobs* with Mike Rowe for a whole weekend, did you think about how doing something with your hands could be really rewarding?

Once you start to discover why you wanted to study abroad so badly or why you were the only one of your friends to finish Girl Scouts, other things in your life will start to make more sense.

- Maybe you played a sport because you always liked the idea of being on a team.
- Maybe you get so angry when others don't recycle because you care so much about the environment.
- Maybe you always go to the same local coffee shop because loyalty is important to you, even if the coffee isn't that great.
- Maybe you rescued a dog from a shelter because you like fighting for things that can't fight for themselves.

Think about the trends in your life or when you feel most alive. What is it about that moment that gives you so much energy? When you discover something you love doing for others, you can find a way to infuse that in different corners of your life.

Someone who loves organizing and making things clean can offer that skill set to their office or start a side hustle as an organizer. Someone who loves making people laugh could come up with ways to make their cold-call customers laugh on the phone. Someone who loves making people feel included could start a neighborhood game night or make sure everyone in the office has someone to eat lunch with.

Purpose is an overlap between what you love doing and what you want to give to others. Discovering your purpose doesn't mean you have to drop everything and start a company or a nonprofit that is aligned with that, but find ways to live a purpose-driven life in what you're doing right now.

When we're captivated by purpose, our willpower is at an all-time high. In fact, we don't even realize it because when work is intentional, it doesn't feel like a task. People ask me about the moment I said yes to starting Headbands of Hope. To be honest, when I think about it, it wasn't a moment of going for it. It was like a piece of paper getting swept up in the wind. I didn't let myself have a moment where I weighed all the pros and cons; instead I just let myself get caught in the flow of purpose.

But you know when an *actual* piece of paper gets caught in the wind and you stomp your foot on top of it to keep it from flying away? Sometimes we do the same thing to our thoughts. We stomp on them with negativity or fear or doubt before we even give ourselves the chance to flow with it. Sure, maybe we'll start rolling with something and realize some obstacles we didn't think about, but we're much more likely to find work-arounds after we've already started rather than before we even begin.

ANCHOR YOUR PURPOSE

Remember when I was chasing a magazine cover and anything that was shiny? Where was my purpose then? Even when you start with great intentions, it's easy for your purpose to get lost as things build and more noise surrounds what you're doing, which is why we need to anchor it.

When you drop an anchor into the water, it has to be heavy in order to work. It's the same with our beliefs; they have to be heavily weighted by something that is worth fighting for, or else the rough seas will be enough reason for us to drift away. And once we have an idea that aligns deeply with our purpose, we feel anchored.

I keep a file on my computer that is my anchor point. It's a file of all the pictures and letters we've received over the years from patients and families and hospital staff. When I open that file, I feel my anchor dig in to the seafloor.

Right now if I open up that file I'll see:

- A picture from our latest DIY Headband Day at Duke, where a girl and I are trying to balance markers on top of our lips.
- A picture of a patient who just finished chemo wearing her headband.
- A thank-you letter from Nationwide Children's Hospital.
- A picture of a childhood cancer camp that just got a box of headbands for their campers.
- A letter from a high school student who researched me for a project and is now starting her own social business because she was inspired by mine.
- A picture of the Dallas Mavericks cheerleaders passing out headbands in the children's hospital.

And I need that because every once in a while I'll start to drift and chase shiny things or start to question what I'm doing. I do the same thing for my other ventures too. For Mic Drop Workshop, I created a file of screenshots of women at their first gig, or a standing ovation after their speeches, or notes that they finally feel confident to tell their story.

These files are collections of the reasons why I started. They're what I hoped these ventures would produce. But sometimes the rough waters of growth can make it harder to see the shore you started from. And when you can't see where you've started, you don't know how far you've come. It can be hard to always put purpose first, which is why it needs to be an active conversation that you revisit and keep dropping anchors.

Whatever reminds you of why your actions matter are your anchor points. Make a list, save files, put it close to you. Take the time to build your anchor because you never know when you'll need to revisit it.

ACTIVATE YOUR PURPOSE

In this book, we've talked about certain ingredients needed in the recipe for optimism: ambition, creativity, confidence, and grit. But real talk: I'm not walking through the world with my laundry list of what I need to be that day. I'm not walking up to the office like, "Jess, remember to be ambitious, creative, confident, and resilient today." That sounds exhausting. And if we're focusing so much on what we're supposed to be, we're not leaving enough time or energy to be ourselves.

So let me free you from your laundry list of everything you feel like you have to be, because the one thing that we can focus on that flips on the switch for everything else is our purpose.

If we can activate our purpose, then we will be more confident, relentless, creative, resilient, ambitious, and all of these other qualities that we're trying to practice that push us forward. We can spend so much effort trying to be more creative or trying to be more ambitious, but what if we didn't have to try that hard? Instead of focusing on the dance, we could listen to the music.

Activating our purpose means bringing it to the forefront of our motives and efforts. When you discover what matters to you, it opens the door for you to pursue new ways to chase it down. It highlights different ways you can bring meaning to the surface in what you're doing right now. The best decisions and actions are purposefully charged. However, your purpose is not something that is engraved in your headboard or a picture in your locket, it's how you're actively interpreting the world and your place in it. How you approach your job, your family, your friends, and what you choose to do with each minute of your day.

When you discover how to build your purpose into your work, your work becomes a service, not a job. The hustle becomes organic. The alarm clock becomes a welcomed start to the day, not the end of sleep. The tasks become meaningful. The little moments seem big. The outcomes feel like they moved mountains. And you're walking with a vision of how things could be better, because it matters to you. In other words, you're leading with optimism.

Optimism is taking all of our experiences and choosing to write a good story. But I laugh a little bit when I look back on the past ten years, from my uncle's crash to Headbands of Hope to now. I laugh because none of it was in "the plans." None of it was on my vision board, but somehow it was exactly what I needed. Even if I had the power to change the past, I wouldn't piece it together any differently—except maybe I would have invested in some Bitcoin or not sold all my Beanie Babies too early on eBay.

Having the idea to bring headbands to kids with cancer with no experience or knowledge to support it taught me that everything we believe in is within our reach if it's driven by purpose. When something matters enough, we activate parts of ourselves we didn't know we had. We can stop attaching our confidence to what skills or knowledge we know, and instead attach it to what we know we can do. Because if it's meaningful enough, you bet your booty we will figure it out.

Everything we want is within reach if we're willing to throw perfection out the door and embrace the messiness of the journey.

We can see our future in two ways: a scary mess of uncontrollable experiences or plentiful opportunities to write our own stories. And optimism is just about choosing to write a good story for yourself, for others, for the world . . . or whatever a good story means to you. In order for us to have a chance at making a dent on the universe, we have to be optimistic enough to see something better and confident enough to just begin.

My story started with a headband.

How will yours begin?

NOTES

1. Kendra Cherry, "Benefits of Positive Thinking for Body and Mind," Verywell Mind, updated June 21, 2019, https://www.verywellmind.com /benefits-of-positive-thinking-2794767.
2. "Optimism and Your Health," *Harvard Men's Health Watch*, Harvard Health Publishing: Harvard Medical School, May 2008, https://www .health.harvard.edu/heart-health/optimism-and-your-health.
3. C. Conversano, A. Rotondo, E. Lensi, O. Della Vista, F. Arpone, and M. A. Reda, "Optimism and Its Impact on Mental and Physical Well-Being," *Clinical Practice and Epidemiology in Mental Health: CP & EMH*, 6 (May 2010): 25–29, https://benthamopen.com/FULLTEXT/CPEMH-6-25.
4. Todd Rose and Ogi Ogas, *Dark Horse: Achieving Success Through the Pursuit of Fulfillment* (New York: HarperOne, 2018).
5. Barbara Corcoran (@BarbaraCorcoran), Twitter, December 27, 2018, 4:01 a.m., https://twitter.com/BarbaraCorcoran/status/10782594 64988430337.
6. Blake Richardson, "Talk Your Way to Success: Self-Talk and the Power of Flexible Thinking," Connected Coaches, May 29, 2018, https://connected coaches.org/spaces/10/welcome-and-general/blogs/general/14330/talk-your -way-to-success-self-talk-and-the-power-of-flexible-thinking.
7. "How Language Impacts Your Health and Fitness: Channeling Your Self Talk + Inner Voice," Fitness on the Run, https://fitnessontherun.net /channeling-self-talk-inner-voice/.
8. Richardson, "Talk Your Way to Success."
9. "How Language Impacts Your Health and Fitness."

10. Nir Eyal, "Have We Been Thinking About Willpower the Wrong Way for 30 Years?" *Harvard Business Review*, November 23, 2016, https://hbr .org/2016/11/have-we-been-thinking-about-willpower-the-wrong-way-for -30-years.

11. Eyal, "Have We Been Thinking About Willpower."

12. Dictionary.com, s.v. "purpose (*n*.)," accessed June 26, 2019, https://www .dictionary.com/browse/purpose.

ACKNOWLEDGMENTS

Ironically, when I needed optimism the most, it was the process of writing this book. There were moments when my optimism was rattled, and I wasn't sure this was going to happen for me. But then I met Bob Goff backstage when I was speaking at Catalyst University and he introduced me to my wonderful agents, Karen and Curtis Yates. Thank you both for seeing this book before I even saw it. Thank you for believing in me as a new author and seeing the path ahead, not just where I was standing. You are the people who made me believe I'm an author.

To my team at Headbands of Hope. Lauren, thank goodness we were roommates freshman year. Don't know how I'd get by without you. We've come a long way from driving to Delaware and having meetings with our dads at the table, but there's no one I'd rather come that long of a way with! Caroline, you are a light in my life and always will be. Thank you for always making me smile. Brittany, anytime you fall from a table, I'll be here to catch you. I'm so happy life continued to bring us together all these years. Mark, thanks for being my therapist—I mean business advisor. Josh, you saw potential in me before I saw it in myself. Thank you for being way more than just a "tech guy." Lily, I like to think I live life ten steps ahead. If that's true, then you live life fifteen steps ahead and encourage me to keep up. You're a rockstar. Cathy, thank you for keeping me organized and being my cheerleader. Samantha and Dana, thank you both for holding it down at the warehouse and sending out hope all around the world. Michelle, meeting you was a turning point in my life and we're only going up from here!

To the team at W Publishing. Megan, you're my soul sister. Thanks for believing in this book and bringing it to life, despite that you start your car with a screwdriver. Daisy, I knew from the moment we first spoke on the phone that you were special, and every interaction I've had with you has proved that right. Sam and Dawn, thanks for making this book the best it can be. Kristi and Becky, you make the magic happen, and I'm so grateful.

James Robilotta, thank you for bringing my punchlines from a 7 to a 10. This book is so much better because of you. Antonio Neeves, when I had my first speech at Lander, you were there. You said afterward, "Cross it off as a win and don't look back." I've been living my life like that ever since. Thanks for being my friend. Kristen Hadeed, my speaker sister. Thank you for paving the way and being there for me. Bobby Martin, thank you for pushing me to write this book. Maybe it was you or maybe it was the beer, but either way, thank you.

Lisa Friedman, thank you for making me an author years ago and for investing in young writers. Mark Dunn, I heard you saying "show, don't tell" as I was writing this book. Thanks for pouring kerosene on my love for writing. Monty Coggins, thank you for teaching me it's noble and courageous to ask for help. Mindy Sopher, if I live my life with half as much love and zest as you do, I'll cross it off as a win. Dr. De Moya, thanks for letting me pursue my dreams while I was in your class. To other teachers that shaped me: Angie Borjes, Diana Hyman, Becky Deal, Ginger Holloway, Lisa Craig, Ryan Hurley, thank you for being so instrumental in my life.

Maggie Kane, thanks for all the free coffee and pastries at A Place at the Table when I was writing this book. You have a heart of gold, and I'm honored to be your friend. Emily and Amanda, thank you for always being there for me, even when it's on a cruise ship in Mexico. Kate Gremillion and Ashley Beaudin, you both keep me sane and inspire me. To all my girls: Taylor Ekman, Kenly Dine, Katie Kahut, Marina Randles, Magdalyn Duffie, Leslie Woods, Liz Tracy, Katelyn Kennedy.

Thank you all for being so much light to my life and supporting me during this process.

To John and Teresa Kahut, I hit the jackpot when it comes to in-laws. Teresa, thanks for letting me love your son and welcoming me into the family. John, thanks for not kicking me out after Flight Simulator.

To my wonderful grandparents: Tina, you taught me to see the world in color with your art. Joan, you taught me to stand up for what I want, educate myself, and put froth in my coffee. Bob, you taught me to put maple syrup on my cereal and that if it's not broken you can still try to fix it.

To my family: my sister, Heather, my dad, Rich, and my mom, Laurie. Man, where do I even begin? Thank you for giving me a life that has been messy but neat. Challenging but fun. Crazy yet sane. Hard but easy. Risky but always safe. Thank you for supporting my dreams, whether that was filming my "music videos" in the garage or writing this book. Everything I do has all of your fingerprints all over it.

And lastly, to my husband, Jake. Years ago I was frustrated about something work-related and I said something along the lines of: *I can't do XYZ right now because I'm too frustrated.* And you looked at me and said, "That's fine, but you can also choose not to be." You've taught me many things (like how to hitch up an Airstream and make nachos with Doritos), but teaching me that I have the control of how I walk through life is one of the biggest gifts you've ever gifted me. And I know that I always want to walk through life with *you.* Thank you for being my bright side. I love you.

ABOUT THE AUTHOR

JESS EKSTROM is the founder and CEO of Headbands of Hope, which to date has donated more than half a million headbands to every children's hospital in the United States and hospitals in fifteen additional countries. Jess is also a professional speaker and founder of Mic Drop Workshop, an online course with the mission of empowering more women to share their message as speakers. She lives in Raleigh, North Carolina, with her husband and standard poodle, Ollie.

LET'S TALK ABOUT IT

CHAPTER ONE: MAYBE
SHE'S BORN WITH IT

- As a kid, what kind of optimistic beliefs did you have? What did you dream for the future?
- Jess says, "But then something happens that pops our balloon." What life experience caused you to lose some of your childlike optimism?
- What would you do if you weren't concerned about the chance of failure?

CHAPTER TWO: ANYTHING CAN HAPPEN

- Discuss a time in your life that shook your worldview.
- What does Jess suggest is the difference between experiences and stories? Discuss some examples of uncontrollable experiences in your life in which you controlled the story.
- What is your story now, and how has it changed?

CHAPTER THREE: YES, AND . . .

- Was there a time when you let the "but" get in the way of your "yes"? How did that affect your situation?
- Not knowing the end result or being fully prepared for something

can be scary. Describe a time when you said yes to something new and how you felt. Did you get that "oh, crap" feeling, and if so, how did you deal with it?

- If you could say yes to any job in the world, what would it be? Practice saying and completing the phrase, "Yes, and . . ."

CHAPTER FOUR: IF IT ISN'T THERE, CREATE IT

- Jess says hard times can be the excuse to do less or the reason to do more. Name some hard times that you've experienced or seen that produced more.
- What limiting beliefs do you have about yourself? How can you reframe those as possibilities?
- Who or what inspires you the most? How can these inspirations drive you to create a better world?

CHAPTER FIVE: BABY STEPS

- What are examples of small actions on a to-do list that give you satisfaction? Why does completing these tasks make you feel good?
- Describe a time when you had to be resourceful in order to accomplish a goal.
- What daunting dream do you have, and what is one small action could you do today to work toward that dream?

CHAPTER SIX: SHE MADE IT WORK

- Share your own "She made it work" story.
- On page 65, Jess talks about transparency and other people's

transparency. What are the advantages of being transparent? Is it hard for you to be honest?

- Can you share a time when you were rejected? What did you do after? Would you change anything?

CHAPTER SEVEN: THROW A FAIL MARY

- Have you ever been in a situation in which you wished you had spoken up? Or you did speak up? What was the result of that? How can using your voice change the dynamics?
- Jess says, "We don't become successful from avoiding failures; we become successful when we're strong enough to navigate them" (83). What are some failures you have experienced?
- What has been your biggest failure? What has been your biggest success? How have your failures contributed to your successes, and vice versa?

CHAPTER EIGHT: YOU'RE TALL ENOUGH

- Describe a time when you felt unqualified and how you overcame it.
- Was there a time when you took a bad experience and turned it into a new story about yourself?
- In what area can you start "asking for the ball" even when you're not fully ready?

CHAPTER NINE: FINDING THE WHITE SPACE

- Describe a time when you compared yourself to someone else. How did it make you feel? How often do you compare yourself to others?

- What do you think drives us to measure ourselves against other people?
- If you had your own individuality metric, how would you measure success?

CHAPTER TEN: THE WORST FUND-RAISER EVER

- How have you been "silently fulfilled" by lending a helping hand?
- In what ways can you lead with compassion and action at work, at school, at home, at the gym, and so forth?
- Describe a time when someone did something nice for you. Why do you think acts of kindness or generosity are so impactful?

CHAPTER ELEVEN: THE THINGS WE TELL OURSELVES

- What songs would be on your morning hype playlist?
- When you wake up in the morning, how do you choose to start your day? What is a phrase you can say aloud to direct the course of your day?
- Describe a time when you had to "figure it out."

CHAPTER TWELVE: THE STRUGGLE IS WORTH IT

- Are you comfortable publicly displaying negative emotions, like crying or yelling? Do you face your emotions head on, or do you hide them?
- Do you think feeling pain is showing weakness? Why or why not?
- Has pain or discomfort caused you to take action? What did you do?

CHAPTER THIRTEEN: ALIGNMENT
OVER ATTENTION

- The author talks about alignment vs. attention on page 173. In what ways have you experienced the difference between alignment and attention in your life? What are some ways you feel "inner applause"? What are some ways you experience "outer applause"?
- Do you tend to find more value in attention or alignment, and why?
- "Fulfillment is not a destination we reach through achievements, it's a choice on how we live our lives right now" (180). How do you choose to live your life? What is it you plan to do with your one life?

CHAPTER FOURTEEN: ACTIVATE YOUR PURPOSE

- What is something you find meaningful? What gives you hope? What wakes you up every morning and keeps you up at night? What makes you put in the work?
- How have you experienced "organic hustle"?
- What is your anchor? What helps you feel grounded? What helps you stay focused on your purpose and vision?

A Note from Jess

Did you think we'd just leave it like that? Like we had a beautiful date and I never called you again? Like that deep conversation and shared plate of calamari meant nothing? Think again.

For better or for worse, you're officially in the tribe! I've created some reader exclusive surprises for you that you can access below. And please keep in touch with me on social, I'd love to hear from you!

UNLOCK READER EXCLUSIVE:

Chasingthebrightside.com
Enter the code: HOPE

CONNECT WITH ME ON SOCIAL:

Instagram: @jess_ekstrom
Twitter: @jess_ekstrom
Facebook: @jessekstrom
#chasingthebrightside

For speaking inquiries + to sign up
for my email list, please head to:
JessEkstrom.com

To shop and learn more about
Headbands of Hope, please head to:
headbandsofhope.com